WHY PRIESTS?

Brilliant, controversial and outspoken, no single voice championing freedom within the Catholic Church has attracted more universal attention than that of Hans Küng. The 45-year-old Swiss-born Professor of Dogmatic and Ecumenical Theology and Director of the Institute of Ecumenical Studies at Tübingen University in West Germany was one of the select group of official theologians appointed during Vatican II Council by Pope John himself. Known as 'the young protégé of modern theology', Küng has for a number of years been highly thought of for his theological knowledge and insight not only among Catholics but also by theologians of all denominations. Immensely popular among, and the hero of, the progressives, his outspoken statements on birth control, mixed marriages and celibacy of the clergy have already 'fired some people with great enthusiasm and others with apoplectic antagonism'. Throughout his stormy career, he has been involved in one imbroglio after another with various congregations in the Holy See. He has written several books; among them: *The Council, Reform and Reunion, The Church* (dedicated to the Archbishop of Canterbury), and *Infallible?*

HANS KÜNG

WHY PRIESTS?

Translated from the German
by John Cumming

COLLINS

FONTANA LIBRARY OF
THEOLOGY AND PHILOSOPHY

First published under the title
Wozu Priester? by Benziger Verlag, 1971
First published in the English translation
by The Fontana Library of Theology and Philosophy, 1972

Original German edition © Copyright 1971 Benziger Verlag
English translation © Copyright 1972
by William Collins Sons & Co Ltd, London

Printed in Great Britain
Collins Clear-Type Press
London and Glasgow

CONTENTS

As a help to my brothers . . .

FOREWORD

I wrote this essay because:

1. I was concerned about the dire situation of priests in the Catholic Church and in the other Christian Churches, as something that I have been faced with constantly and in a variety of ways. The loss rate and, above all, the decline in vocations not only in North and South America but in Europe are clear evidence that the crisis is approaching disaster point.

2. The official documents issued hitherto by the bishops, and by Rome in particular, do not seem to fit the extremity of the case.

3. The third and ineffectual synod of bishops (Rome, Autumn 1971) confirmed our fears that the bishops would fail to respond to the present unhappy situation. Recently the gulf (for which there is statistical evidence in the United States) between the traditionally Rome-oriented bishops and a great number of priests—not always the young ones, by a long way—has widened quite ominously.

In this situation an individual theologian can surely do no more than use his insight into the state of Church and society and his profound concern with the original New Testament witness, the tradition of the Church and modern theology, in an attempt to give a contemporary but essentially Christian, fundamental and—one hopes—practical answer to the question, 'Why priests?'

I do not think my answer could be thought destructive, even though it avoids the theological compromise so often resorted to, and ruthlessly discards some now untenable traditional ideas. As the prophet says, one must try to sow as well as to pluck up. My efforts have been directed wholly to giving a constructive answer that would enable curate, parish priest or bishop honestly to serve the Church authorities at the present time.

The older ones among us need help. They came up in a specific tradition and are unwilling to see all they believed and all they did for so many years—indeed, the greater part of their lives—appear as so much dust. But the younger clergy also need help. They can no longer accept some of the old assurances; they expect more substantial evidence and less equivocal discourse; they have the various ingredients of a new answer to hand, but are possibly unable to find the right recipe. To them I would say: we need an impartial study of what ought to stay and what ought to go; of where steadfastness is requisite and where change. We must preserve continuity in the midst of all discontinuity, yet (no easy task) not fear discontinuity in the midst of continuity.

No one can escape the rethinking process at a time when one epoch is passing into another. We scarcely dare to predict how the Church will look in ten years' time. Rethinking is not easy. To have written works of theology for some fifteen years which were at first variously resisted but in the end widely accepted is to have gained much experience in this regard. But, in terms of the question I have posed, rethinking means an opportunity for better understanding and work for service to the gospel and to mankind.

It should be obvious that the only meaningful answer to a question about the ministry of the Church is an ecumenical one. Protestant questions (do we really need any special ecclesiastical ministry, any ministers, or any ordination?) and the answers of Protestant theologians have been given full consideration. If the answer proposed here happens to prevail in the Catholic Church, there should be nothing in the way of ecumenical understanding on this point. The practical consequences would be immense: there would be no obstacle to a mutual recognition of ministries, and the major barrier on the way to intercommunion and eucharistic communion would be removed.

This is not to imply that the present essay offers *the* answer to the question. It is only *one* answer; but one that is the fruit of mature consideration since the first year of Vatican II and the debates on Chapter 3 of the Constitution on the Church, by way of my work *The Church* (where the interested reader will find the ecclesiological bases for this study), up to the latest discussion on the ecclesiastical ministry.

There has been much to thank many people for over these years: not least certain valuable corrections which I owe to the study-group of the ecumenical university institutes in Germany. The third chapter of the present essay derives from the stimulus of a bulletin of the Munich University Institute, directed by Professors Heinrich Fries and Wolfhart Pannenberg (cf. *Una Sancta*, 25 [1970], pp. 107-15). The entire work has been tried out in the course of several doctoral colloquia at Tübingen. During my last reworking of the manuscript, I have been most indebted to my closest co-workers (also my most telling critics): Drs Hermann Häring, Friedhelm Krüger, Josef Nolte and Margret Gentner.

The very favourable reception accorded it by some hundreds of parish priests and chaplains at lectures in Tübingen and in the Bavarian Catholic Academy encouraged me to publish the essay. Therefore I dedicate it to my brothers in the ministry. During my recent lecture tour round the world, I was able to experience for myself what Paul meant when he said, 'I want to bring you some spiritual strength, and that will mean that I shall be strengthened by you, each of us helped by the other's faith' (Rom. 1: 11-12).

Hans Küng
New York, November 1971

THE QUESTION

The crisis in the ministry of the Church is a complex one. It reaches from the biblical foundations to the actual exercise of that ministry. The responsibility may be traced both to the general process of secularization and democratization and to the particular uncertainty about function that attaches to the ministry (rôle conflict and communication problems in the parish, a one-track exercise of office, a lack of guidelines for the future, the training of priests, and the law of celibacy). We are forced to put the question quite radically—to ask: *Why priests?* What can a special 'ministry' really mean in the Church today? In a pluralist and democratic society, what does it mean to have such a distinction between minister and people, between 'high' and 'low', between those who talk and those who listen, those who give and those who carry out the orders, those who bestow and those who receive? Of course the question can be put the other way round: given modern, democratic forms of thought and of society, and the claims of industrial, pluralist and democratic society to as high a degree of co-determination as possible, to self-affirmation through achievement, and to specialization by means of a systematic division of labour, are not distinctive offices in the Church excluded from the start?

If the question of the functions and effective action of ministries is to receive not a vague and arbitrary answer, but one proficiently grounded in regard to the church community, we must answer both the question about the origin and that about the legitimation of these offices. Insofar as ecclesial offices are matters of human communication and interaction, *social developments* at a certain time necessarily affect the way in which one understands the ministry. But, inasmuch as an ecclesial office claims to be Christian, the fundamental data of Christianity have to be taken into account. This means, in fact, that we can never disregard the figure that (for the historian), as the historically actual Jesus of Nazareth, is the beginning of the Church and at the same time (for the theologian), as the Christ of God and object of faith, its still normative origin.

What, as far as the historian is concerned, took place in Jesus 'at one particular time' is something that, for the faith of the community, is valid 'for all time'. Nothing can be certified as 'Christian' except it derive from Jesus; and the Church cannot represent itself as the Church of Christ if it does not come from him. The Church, its credibility and efficiency in our society, stand or fall according to whether it is the location and memorial of Jesus, it defends the cause of Jesus Christ in private and in public, and in the world and society of today remains— despite all omissions of word and deed—the representative of Jesus Christ.

Only on this basis is it possible to recognize the permanent essence of ecclesial 'offices' as it has persisted throughout all changing forms and despite all disorders, and to discern the variables and constants in historical actuality. Accordingly, any reflection on the 'priesthood', on an ecclesial 'office' which claims to be Christian, must constantly refer to the original, basic documentation of Christian faith and life: the Old and New Testament writings, which compelled recognition from the Church as the authentic, original tradition of Jesus Christ, and are always to be consulted on this their essential concern.

One

THE CHURCH AS A COMMUNITY IN FREEDOM, EQUALITY AND FRATERNITY

I. DEMOCRATIZATION OF THE CHURCH?

A few preliminary remarks are necessary here. *Today* the question of church ministry arises in the perspective of the problematic notions of 'democratization'—the democratization of the Church as well as of society. Democratization is not a panacea for society; it is not the sole principle of social structure, to be applied uniformly and 'indiscriminately' to State, family, economy, culture, and hence the Church. Democracy is not a univocal concept which can be used in the same way for a form of government, an engineering works, a schoolroom, a theatre or a ship. Only totalitarian means (and perhaps not even those, if the experiences of our century are anything to go by) could allow a wholly co-ordinated process of democratization (economic, political, educational and social). Like democracy itself, democratization is an analogous and even ambiguous concept that only history can make specific; in theology it can be used at best only for a critical interpretation and differentiation based on the standard (the *norma normans*) of the New Testament message.

Democratization of the Church cannot mean replacing the power of its ministers by the power of the people (in the sense of a direct sovereignty of the people). Even in the case of Abraham Lincoln's fine definition, 'government of the people, by the people and for the people,' the phrase 'by the people' has given rise to considerable controversy, whereas the 'New Left'—interpreting it as 'representative democracy' (which allows of only an indirect form of 'government by the people')—rejects it completely. A differentiated democratization will certainly not be content with the objective of *formal* democracy (in the sense of an inconsequential institution). On the other hand, it will not strive for a *total* democratization (for an illusory equalization).

A differentiated democratization of the Church, which *a priori* can have no other goal than the best possible democracy, intends a growing co-responsibility of *all* members of the ecclesial community by means of *appropriate* shared decisions in freedom and solidarity for the good of the whole and of each individual. A democratization of this kind does not desire a violent upheaval of the values and leadership of the Church, but a dynamic *process* by means of which, at all levels of the Church (from the 'top', in the institutions of the world Church, to the 'bottom', in the parishes; in macro-structures and in micro-structures) a form of life (and not a form of domination) will be produced both in ways of thinking (principles, attitudes, style, behaviour patterns) and in the institution and its structure (constitutional, organizational and legal forms). This, it is hoped, will correspond more adequately than the previous one to the Christian message itself and to the modern idea of the greatest possible degree of freedom and the best possible form of (legal) equality. This full human self-realization and association of power and rule with the common good, justice and a popular consensus without coercion, owe as much to the Greek conception of the 'city' (the *polis* as the common concern of all citizens) and to Roman legal theory (the maxim '*quod omnes tangit, ab omnibus tractari debet*'), as to impulses and motives of Christian origin—which deserve some short consideration.

In this context, I ought, perhaps, to stress the fact that the democratic slogans of the French Revolution were not *a priori* hostile to the Church. Despite their other ingredients, they were originally Christian watchwords. From the start they had an inward, 'spiritual' *and* a social dimension. But their preferred modern application to the social and political sphere in the sense of democratization—opposed to the absolutism of the *Ancien Régime* (which was not exactly Christian)—accorded with the age. The Catholic Church and, to a large extent, the other Churches, did not understand this at the time because they themselves were too far from the original evangelical liberty, equality and fraternity. Hence, in the moment of truth, they were unable to recognize their adult children in these illegitimate offspring. Today there is all the more reason to take these and similar democratic slogans (solidarity and participation, human dignity and the rights of man, individual responsibility and self-determination, shared discussion and co-determination, communication and dialogue), and to establish their Christian foundation and content for the community of believers: to show what they actually stand for, and to put them right. On the other hand, such Christian concepts as *koinonia*, communion and charity must be analysed, in order to give them the social reference appropriate to our times. And Christians more than others have to avoid any false modesty when doing this.

In a wholly Christian perspective, of course, we can no longer view the Church as the bastion of anti-democratic reaction that it still seems to be for quite a few, even in Europe. On the other hand, the Church must not surrender uncritically to any progressive movement that hoists the democratic ensign; it must beware of becoming a political party, of not keeping its proper distance, and of substituting a politics of the 'left' for its former adherence to the 'right'.

No, in a time of 'fundamental democratization' (of society and of the State), the Church ought to express its essential content—the Christian message which is both proclamation and active aid—in an unequivocally critical yet constructive manner. Then it might again become the major advocate and defender of humanity in our so often inhuman society. For in this Church there still burns something of the goodness and loving-kindness of God to man, and something too of the new humanity of man. As a non-dominative and non-coercive community, the Church could be a model of the best possible form of democracy: and show that, as things are now developing, a differentiated form of democracy is very necessary; but that juridical control, legal measures and institutional optimization are by no means adequate components of 'fundamental democratization'. At the same time it could refer to that great plan (*real utopia*) to which it owes its own existence, and which has served as a tacit norm (or even explicit motivation) for non-Christian or anti-Christian political movements: all men living in freedom and brotherhood in a perfect community of peace, love and justice (communication free from domination; and a universal consensus without constraint), as promised, in conformity with Jesus' word, by the Christian proclamation of the Church as the kingdom of God—God all in all.

In this perspective, that which is specifically Christian—belief in the Crucified—is essentially concerned with depths that no secular social criticism has ever managed to plumb. It would have men take the initiative and *act* in science, economics, politics, government, law and culture. But it also enables men to hold on even where there is no advance, and where no social evolution or socialist revolution can overcome the tensions and contradictions of human life and society. Even in conditions of profound injustice, even in servitude and discord, Christian faith enables men not to despair of peace, liberty and justice. It allows hope to penetrate even where there is nothing left to hope for; a love to persist that includes even one's enemy; and work to be done for the humanization of man and society, even where men are busy spreading inhumanity.

2. THE CHURCH AS A COMMUNITY OF BELIEVERS

Democratization (in our differentiated sense—if you dislike the word, replace it with another) is universally recommended these days, and rightly so; but as far as the Church is concerned it cannot be an uncritical adaptation to the spirit of the times. The Church's responsibility is to the gospel of Jesus Christ. And a Church that bears the name of Jesus, heeds his word, and is impelled by his Spirit, must never be identified with a particular class, caste, clique or bureaucracy. Like Jesus himself, his Church addresses people as a whole, and expressly the underprivileged. Hence the Church is the entire *community* of those who believe in Christ, in which *all* may look upon themselves as the people of God, the body of Christ and the temple of the Spirit. The decisive criterion for membership in this case is not some privilege of birth, rank, race or office. The specific factor is not that one enjoys an 'office' in the Church (and the kind of 'office' it is); what matters is that one is a 'believer' pure and simple: that is, a person who believes, listens, serves, loves and hopes.

In contradistinction to the pagan or Jewish cult, a Christian does not need the mediation of a priest in order to enter the innermost sanctuary of his temple: that is, to reach God himself. On the contrary, he is admitted to the ultimate immediacy of God, which no church authority can spoil, or forbid him. As far as decisions taken in this most private of spheres are concerned, neither judgment nor the power to dispose nor the power to command belongs to any individual. Admittedly the Christian faith does not fall straight from heaven; it comes by way of the Church. But the 'Church' is the *total* community which, announcing the gospel—often more by way of the unimportant than through hierarchs and theologians, more by actions than by words—awakens faith in Jesus Christ, evokes commitment to his Spirit, makes the Church present in the world in the form of everyday Christian witness, and promotes the cause of Jesus Christ. All and not just a few of the elect are entrusted with the proclamation of the Christian message, are required to live an individual and social life on the basis of the gospel, are baptized in the name of Jesus, receive the memorial Supper of thanks and the covenant, are open to the words of forgiveness, and are charged with everyday service, and with responsibility for their neighbour, the community and the world. In all these basic functions of the Church, there is communion in liberty, equality and fraternity.

3. FREEDOM

Freedom is both gift and commission for the Church. The Church can and should bring into being a *community of free men*. The Church represents Jesus Christ and must never be a repressive institution or a Grand Inquisition. Its members are liberated to freedom: freed from slavery to the letter of the law, from the burden of guilt, from fear of death; liberated for life, service and love: men subject only to God and not to anonymous powers or to other men. Of course faith in the crucified Lord cannot and does not intend any abolition of right and power in society: the kingdom of total liberty has not yet come. But this faith effectively circumscribes right and power and relativizes them radically. Faith in the Crucified makes man so free in the order of right, that he becomes capable—through love of another—of surrendering a right without any recompense, and even of going two miles with one who had asked only for a mile. It makes men so free in the social struggle for power that they are capable, for the sake of another, of using power to their own cost, and thus of giving away their coat with their tunic.

The Christian message, or, in other words, the values of the Sermon on the Mount as authenticated by the life and death of Jesus, would not establish a new law, or instal a new order of rights. The values of Jesus want *liberation from the law*. The Spirit of the Lord is absent where there is no liberty. However important the realization of this liberty may be in an individual life, its relevance in the Church cannot remain merely that of a moral exhortation (for the most part addressed to others). It is to be exercised on the forms taken by the Christian community, on its institutions and constitutions, in such a way that the latter are never oppressive or repressive. Given this basic freedom of the children of God, no one in the Church has any right to manipulate it, to suppress it or to abolish it, whether openly or secretly; and there is no one with the right to supplant the reign of God with man's domination over man. It is this liberty which ought to be apparent in the Church in terms of free speech (openness), of free choice of action or abstention (the freedom to come and go, liberality in the widest sense), and also of ecclesial institutions and constitutions. The Church itself should be both the *location of liberty* and the *advocate of liberty in the world*.

In such a community of free individuals, all members without distinction would then be able, thanks to the light and power of Jesus, to retain their liberty in the world of today, despite its constraints (the slavery of the economy, of science, of the State), despite 'idols' (the personality cult) and false gods (the worship of riches, pleasure and power). Imbued with faith in God the creator of the world, without enmity, and free from alienation, they would serve this world, confident that history has a meaning and—once the world is reconciled—a future.

4. EQUALITY

On the basis of a given and realized liberty, the Church will (as it can and must) be a *community of fundamentally equal individuals*; not, of course, in the sense of a levelling down of diverse gifts and functions, but in that of a fundamental equality of rights proper to members who are very different in themselves. Commissioned by Jesus Christ, the Church can never be the Church of one class, race, caste or clergy. It is by virtue of a free decision that each of its members becomes or remains one of the community of faith. It is in a solidarity of love that the unequal, rich and poor, great and small, educated and illiterate, whites and blacks, men and women join together. Faith in the Crucified cannot and does not intend the abolition of all social inequality. The commonwealth of perfect equality is not yet with us. But this faith is also able to 'compensate' and sublate inequalities of social origin (master and slave), of cultural origin (Greeks and barbarians), and natural origin (man and woman). Basically, all members of Church are equal in right: they have the same rights and the same duties.

No personal prestige should be determinative among the people of God; in the body of Christ there is no member so insignificant as to have to suffer contempt. This fundamental equality appertains to each individual, yet in the Church should be more than an inconsequential 'attitude'. The constitutional structures of the ecclesial community should so preserve and protect it as never to favour injustice and exploitation. No one in the Church has the right to suppress the fundamental equality of believers, or to ignore it or falsify it in a domination of men by men. This equality occurs in the Church so that he who is great—the first—makes himself the helper and servant of all, and at the same time the structures of the Church are so constituted as to bear witness to the fundamental equality of its members: the Church itself must be both the dwelling place of the equality of rights and the defender of that equality in the world. In such a community of individuals equal before the law, thanks to the light and power of Jesus, all members can in today's world enjoy a truly human life, activity, suffering and death, because until the last they are supported in everything by God, who has committed himself to man.

5. FRATERNITY

On the basis of a given and actual liberty and equality, the Church can and ought to be a community of brothers and sisters. Commissioned by Jesus Christ, the Church as an institution must never use the patriarchal form of government. In the Church there is only one holy Father: God himself. All members of the Church are his adult sons and daughters who are not to be forced back into immaturity. In this community, the only valid human authority is truly fraternal and not paternalist. There is only one lord and master: Jesus Christ himself. All members of the Church are brothers and sisters. It is not the patriarch who is the norm for this community, but the will of God which, according to Jesus' message, intends the good of men—of all men. In this fraternal community, individual and social misery can find resolution at a level quite different to that possible in the society of consumption and production. Faith in the Crucified makes possible something one cannot ask of man in bourgeois or marxist society, and which is nevertheless of immense importance for all human co-existence, whether between individuals, peoples, languages, races, or Churches: instead of guilt to impute, the ability to forgive indefinitely; instead of positions to defend, the ability to reach unconditional reconciliation; instead of unending litigation, the higher justice of love; instead of unrelenting struggle for power, the peace which passes all understanding. This kind of message is no mere opium of consolation. More radically than other programmes, it points the way into the actuality of the world: it is for change where there is a threat that the ruled will be crushed by their rulers, individuals by institutions, freedom by order, and right by force.

The liberty of Christian brotherhood unites independence and obligation, power and renunciation, autonomy and service, being a master and being a servant—an enigma whose solution is the charity in which the master becomes a servant and the servant a master, obligation becomes independence and independence obligation. Even the basically antithetical democratic demands for the greatest possible liberty and optimal equality can be reconciled in such a brotherhood. This fraternity must be personal and ought not to be reduced to fine words and phrases such as the 'spirit' of brotherhood (more often in fact a spirit of subjection). It has to be realized in social rules and relations that involve no human alienation. No one in the Church has any right to replace this fraternity by a personality cult and the paternalism of a clerical system, and thus to reinforce the domination of man over man. Brotherhood ought to be apparent in the rules of the Church and in the social relations which allow it concrete expression. The Church itself should be the location of fraternity and its advocate in the world.

In such a community of brothers and sisters, all without distinction, thanks to the light and power of Jesus, can now call on God as their Father: the mystery of that love which upholds every man, remits the sinner's guilt, and eventually shows itself victorious over sin and death.

These preliminary remarks on the church community in a democratic age should show that this essay on the church ministry is *not* more concerned with '*office*' than with the *Church*, and merely implies what we are to think about the community of the faithful. Many unresolved questions of church 'office' are unresolved community problems. The crisis of the ministry is in essence a crisis of church structures. It is not permissible to ignore the community of the Church, and to argue directly from the sovereignty of Jesus to a sovereign ecclesial 'ministry'—with all the implications of inalienability and unchangeability involved in such a derivation.

Two

EVIDENCE
OF THE NEW TESTAMENT

I. A MULTIPLICITY OF FUNCTIONS

That the Church is a community in freedom, equality and fraternity does not imply any levelling down or uniformity, but on the contrary demands a polymorphous form of structure allowing diversity, mobility and flexibility. The New Testament takes this as self-evident: on the basis of freedom, equality and fraternity there is a rich and flourishing diversity—of individuals and of functions. This indefinite plurality and differentiation of functions, tasks and ministries shows that talk of *the* ministry does not accord with the biblical texts.

In regard to preaching, the New Testament distinguishes the functions of apostles, prophets, doctors, of those who evangelize and those who exhort; and, as assistant ministries, the functions of deacons and deaconesses, the functions of those who distribute alms, those who care for the sick, those widows who serve the community; and finally, for the administration of the community, the functions of elders, presidents, bishops and pastors. In *all* these activities (and not only in those of the specific 'ministries'), Paul (and his communities are the ones about which we are best informed) perceives gifts of the Spirit and a participation in the full power of the glorified Lord of the Church; in them he sees a vocation, God's call to a certain service in the community: in short, a 'charism'. A charism (1) is not primarily an extraordinary phenomenon, but something everyday; (2) is not reduced to a unique form, but is manifest in various ways; (3) is not reserved to a specific category of individuals, but is a universal fact. *All* service that (whether permanently or not) helps to build the community is for Paul a charism,

25

an *ecclesial* service; for this reason it deserves recognition and obedience. Every service, according to its nature, has a certain authority, if it is directed towards the formation of the community in love.

Hence Paul does not expect unity and order in the Church to come from a cancellation of differences but from the action of the one Spirit who gives *his* charism to all (the rule being 'to each his own'), so that it may be used for the sake of all (the rule being 'united for the sake of all') and exercised subject to the one Lord (the rule being 'obedience to the Lord').

Two main criteria enable the spirits to be distinguished: (1) an authentic charism connects one with Jesus and his kingdom: anyone who has the spirit of God acknowledges Jesus as Lord (an affirmation specific to Christian faith); (2) an authentic charism concerns the community: not miracles but service for the sake of the community is the sign of a true vocation. Hence any service in the Church necessarily implies an attitude of solidarity, collegial agreement, exchange between partners, communication and dialogue.

2. SERVICE IN PLACE OF OFFICE

Even though different functions are mentioned in the New Testament, the question of an ecclesial office (ministry) never arises as a theme. Ecclesial 'office' is not a New Testament notion, but a problematical concept which emerged from later reflections. Logically, and—it is clear—intentionally, when ecclesial function is in question, the New Testament writings avoid secular terms relating to 'office', precisely because they denote a relationship of domination.

A more general term is used instead; in Paul it is often a synonym for charism: a very ordinary and not a religious term, with a vague connotation of lowliness, and thus no possible evocation of any association with any public power, administration, sovereignty, high dignity or function of lords and masters. The word used is '*diakonia*', or service (in its fundamental acceptation, *service at table*). Jesus himself obviously supplied the definitive norm here. It is significant that Jesus' logion on service occurs six times in various pericopes (the quarrel among the disciples, the Last Supper, the washing of feet); the greatest of all is to be the servant (the table servant) of all. Accordingly there could not be among Jesus' disciples either an office constituted solely by right and power and corresponding to the commission of a man with power, or one constituted solely by knowledge and dignity, and corresponding to the office of the doctors of the law.

Of course there is authority in the Church, but there is no legitimate authority other than that established upon service and not on force, prerogatives and privileges, which would *require* service. Were one to formulate the matter more precisely in theological terms, it would be preferable to speak of ecclesial '*service*' rather than of ecclesial 'office'. Admittedly in this case it is not the word that is important but one's interpretation of it: the expression 'service' would be wrongly applied and used as camouflage, were there no concomitant rejection of an exercise of power in the Church.

In contrast to 'office', 'service':

(*a*) is part of the terminology of the New Testament, where its substantial acceptation also finds support;

(*b*) because of its functional value, is not at the mercy of a false institutionalist interpretation;

(*c*) in its usual sense already implies a commission to serve, to which everyone exercising a function may be referred;

(*d*) and is consequently something that can clearly be seen to be abused or misused if that is the case.

It is necessary from the viewpoints of theology and terminology alike to ensure the maintenance of a precise distinction between the terms and to guard against their confusion. *Power* may be put to good or to evil ends. Even in the Church, power cannot just be abolished. But it can be exerted practically and appropriately for the common good. And this inevitable exercise of power is something other than its use as *domination* (by individuals or by groups); in the second case, it is a matter of maintaining a privileged position or of increasing one's own power. In the Church the use of power is justifiable only in regard to *service*, and may be gauged only in terms of service. This power deriving from service is authentic (and primarily inward) power; it is a mandated authority. The antonyms here are not power and service, but the use of power as domination and the use of power as service. The exercise of sovereignty (above all by outward power, right up to the limit case of violence) is the opposite of service; it is the *abuse of power*. We ought really to reject as erroneous the term 'holy rule' (hierarchy) introduced by the pseudo-Dionysius, just as we have given up the use of such terms as 'prince-bishop'. We must certainly also renounce the postures and features of rule and domination.

3. A SERVICE OF LEADERSHIP, NOT A PRIESTHOOD

It is even more surprising that the New Testament uses no expressions corresponding to 'office', and in the context of community functions relies on terms for functions drawn from the secular domain; it never use the word 'priest' in the historical sense of sacrifice ('*hiereus*', '*sacerdos*'), and avoids every cultic and sacred term. This certainly has much to do with the fact that Jesus (himself a layman) introduces the figure of the priest once in all his parables, and then only to reject the particular example chosen (Luke 10: 31). When dignitaries—Jewish or pagan—are in question, the word 'priest' is used, but never applied to those who carry out an ecclesial service. It was only at a late date in the New Testament that Jesus himself, the resurrected and glorified, was thought of as a 'priest', but even then in a way that essentially reversed the priesthood of the old Testament: Jesus remains the unique high priest (representative, or mediator), and the offering of his life, made once and for all, fulfils and abolishes the priesthood of the Old Testament (Epistle to the Hebrews). It was a deduction of the community (1 Peter; Revelation) that the dissolution of the *special* priesthood by the priesthood of a new and eternal High Priest implied the *universal* priesthood of all believers, which is essentially direct access to God, a spiritual sacrifice, proclamation of the word, the fulfilment of baptism, the eucharist and forgiveness of sins, and each man's responsibility for and solidarity with all others. The New Testament shows that the word 'priest'—like 'ecclesiastic' and 'cleric', as a special and exclusive term for anyone responsible for an ecclesial service—ought really to be dispensed with; as far as the New Testament is concerned, all believers are 'priests', 'clerics', or 'ecclesiastics'. The term 'priestly ministry' applied not to all Christians, but only to those entrusted with a specific church service, misrepresents the situation recorded in the New Testament. Only *once* (Rom. 15: 16), and not in a 'cultic' context but in regard to preaching, Paul describes himself (he mentions neither bishops nor presbyters) *figuratively* as a 'liturgist', or official who makes the offering (for the Gentiles!); nothing can be found in this text to support the contention of a *cultic priesthood* of certain specific ministers in the New Testament.

Instead of referring to priesthood (to a 'priestly office', to ordination to the priesthood, and so on), it is preferable to use terms that describe functions. Presidents, bishops, deacons, elders, pastors and leaders are mentioned in the New Testament. Some of these designations which at first were neither cultic nor sacred (bishops, pastors, presbyters, deacons) have been retained—justifiably—together with some later ones (vicar, rector). If a more general term is needed that can be used for all these functions, 'service of leadership' or 'presidency' would seem appropriate (one might speak of the person 'responsible for', or the 'president of', a parish, diocese or local or national church, and so on). Some languages are better endowed in this respect than others, since they can use 'ministerium', 'ministero', 'ministerio', 'ministère' or 'ministry' in contradistinction to the more general 'servitium', 'service', 'servizio', 'servicio'. The word 'priest' ('Priester', 'prêtre', 'presbitero', 'prete'), on the other hand—though traditionally a designation for the cultic and sacral priesthood—originated in the non-cultic title given to the elder—the oldest man—of the community. Essentially—as already happens in some Churches—it may be replaced by 'presbyter' or 'elder'.

4. THE BASIC MINISTRY OF THE APOSTLES

Admittedly, not all services enjoy the same importance in the Church. A primary distinction derives from the fact that, according to Paul, not all ministries or charisms are *permanent, public* services to the community. Certain charisms (for example those of exhorting, consoling, counselling with wisdom or knowledge, and the discernment of spirits) are clearly personal gifts from God: aptitudes or virtues put at the service of others and used as the occasion demands. But other charisms (those of the apostles, of prophets, of doctors, evangelists, deacons, presidents, bishops and pastors) are public community functions—functions established by God and exercised in a permanent and regular manner. In regard to the first type, the New Testament mentions gifts and efficacy most often; but for the second type individuals can be named, for this calling is stable enough to be attached to certain persons who, as apostles, prophets, and so on, are 'established' in the Church.

In connection with this second kind of *special* charismatic service (with, that is, permanent, public ministry to the community), it is permissible to speak of a diaconal or charismatic structure of the Church, which is a particular aspect of its general—and fundamental—structure. But this is only a terminological and not a major distinction.

Among the permanent, public ministries, the New Testament as a whole agrees that the *apostolic ministry* has a basic rôle and value in the Church for all time. The apostles (not confined to the Twelve) were the first witnesses and the first messengers, preceding all church ministries; the Church as whole and each of its members are fundamentally indebted to them. As the first witnesses, the apostles proclaimed the message of Christ, founded and administered the first Churches, and cared for their unity. Therefore the Church is built upon them.

The *basic* apostolic succession is therefore that of the Church in general and, individually, that of each Christian in the Church. It continues while incessantly renewing in practice its accordance with the apostles: it must always conform with the apostolic witness (handed down to us through the New Testament) and display an unbroken continuation of apostolic service (missionary progress in the world and edification of the community). The apostolic succession is primarily a succession to the faith and creed of the apostles, and to apostolic service and life. I shall return later to the question of a *special* 'apostolic succession' of administrative services.

5. VARIOUS FORMS OF COMMUNITY

Jesus established an unambiguous criterion of service for the early church community that nevertheless allowed for considerable variation in practice. On the basis of Jesus' norm and the apostles (in addition to whom, according to Paul, 'prophets' and 'doctors' were also very important for the community), and depending on factors of time and place, diverse rules of life could arise in different communities.

As far as we can judge, those communities established

by the apostolic mandate of Paul that remained freely accountable to the apostle in his function of servant of the gospel were self-governing, as far as order and management, and services and functions necessary for the conduct of their life were concerned. These ministries freely demanded by the community enjoyed an authority that could quite justifiably insist upon obedience. Yet not only the exercise of a specific function, but the mode of service proves the authenticity of a ministry. In the epistles whose attribution is uncontested, Paul never mentions ordination or presbyters. He is clearly quite unaware of an institutionalized office with which one is invested and which is then the only one to carry an obligation of communal service. His churches are communities with open charismatic ministries.

In time (and above all after the apostle's death) a process of institutionalization was inevitable, in the Pauline communities too. The fact that shortly after Paul, and even in the charismatic community of Corinth, a presbyteral-episcopal régime should have been imposed so quickly (even though, it would seem, not without some resistance, cf. 1 Clement), is attributable neither to chance nor to decadence. After the period of apostolic establishment, and a period of waiting for the coming of the Lord, and in the age of post-apostolic organization and extension, everything that could help retain the original tradition necessarily won a special importance. Together with the original scriptural witness, a contribution was made to this end by the special mission conferred by the laying-on of hands (ordination): a mission of service to the apostolic tradition and fulfilment of the traditional ecclesial functions.

In Palestinian tradition, institutionalization began very early with the college of elders and with ordination, which was taken over from Judaism. Acts and the Pastoral Epistles also reveal a progress in the Pauline communities towards institutionalization (ordination). However, in other communities (in the circle of Matthew and John) the structures continued to show so very fraternal a character, that at the end of the New Testament epoch there was (without any break in unity) a considerable and irreconcilable diversity in the constitutions of communities, and in the style (in one case, perhaps, charismatic, in another already institutionalized) of church administrative functions. But we have to ask in this regard: can a special 'apostolic succession' of ministries of leadership be maintained under such conditions?

6. THE APOSTOLIC SUCCESSION OF MINISTRIES OF LEADERSHIP

There is no historical support for the contention that the bishops are the direct and exclusive successors of the apostles (not even of the college of Twelve). However, that alone does not settle the question of the special apostolic succession. As direct witnesses and the first to be sent out by Jesus Christ, the apostles could not *a priori* be replaced or represented by any successors, whoever they might be. But, even though there could be no new apostles, the apostolic mission and the apostolic service were still necessary. Both were assumed by the Church as a whole, which, as a whole, can and should remain the '*Ecclesia apostolica*'.

In the matter of administrative functions, however, these ecclesial ministries (bishops, presbyters or parish ministers may be distinguished from the legal or disciplinary, though not the dogmatic or theological, viewpoint) perpetuate in a special way the apostolic commission to establish and direct the Church, a mission which depends on the preaching of the word. It is also possible and justifiable to speak in a functional sense of a special apostolic succession of various administrative functions in the Church. The *special* 'apostolic succession' of these services consists of an establishment and administration of churches, based on the proclamation of the gospel.

From the exegetical and historical viewpoint, to be sure, there is no question of tracing things back to 'divine institution' or to 'institution by Jesus Christ'; we are faced instead with a long and complex historical development.

(1) The episcopes (presbyters), as distinct from the prophets, doctors and other charismatic ministers, prevailed as the leaders, and finally as those solely responsible for the community (a 'collegiality' of *all* the faithful always leads instead to a collegiality of certain groups of ministers *in contradistinction to* the community, producing a divorcement between 'clergy' and 'laity').

(2) Even though there were originally several episcopes (presbyters) in a community, the monarchical episcopate of one bishop increasingly became the pattern (a collegiality of various episcopes or presbyters was replaced by the collegiality of a bishop and his presbyterium and deacons, so that the separation of 'clergy' from 'laity' became definitive).

(3) As the Church spread from the cities to the countryside, the bishop-president of a community became the president of an entire ecclesiastical region, of a diocese, and so on. It was in regard to bishops in our present sense that the 'apostolic succession' became fixed in the form of lists showing the succession in a quasi-monarchical form (side by side with the collegiality of the bishop and his presbyterium, increasing importance was accorded to the collegiality of monarchical bishops among themselves, and then—though only in the West—with the bishop of Rome).

In this functional and historical perspective, a special 'apostolic succession' of ecclesial ministries for the leadership and establishment of the Church may be affirmed on the following conditions:

(1) Those in charge of Churches, as successors to the apostles by special right, are *a priori* accompanied by other ministers and functionaries, and particularly by those who

succeeded the prophets and teachers ('doctors') of the New Testament and who, acting conjointly with those in charge of Churches, enjoy in their own right an authority which derives from the origins.

(2) The apostolic succession of those in charge of the Church, by the laying-on of hands, is not imparted automatically or mechanically: it presupposes belief, and requires a faith operative in the apostolic spirit. It does not exclude the possibility of deficit and error; therefore it has to be verified by the faithful as a whole.

(3) The apostolic succession of those in charge in the Church must take place in the communion of reciprocal service for the Church and for the world. In one way or another, according to the New Testament conception of the Church, presidents and communities have to collaborate in supervising entry into this apostolic succession of ecclesial ministries of leadership. In most cases this would mean a call from the leaders of the community, with the participation of that community.

(4) In view of the constitution of the Pauline and Gentile Christian churches, there should be a possibility (especially in urgent cases) of other modes of entry to the service of church leadership and the apostolic succession of church leaders: designation by other members of the community, or a spontaneous charism to lead or establish the community. The presbyteral-episcopal form which prevailed in the post-apostolic epoch should—at least in principle—be open today to all the eventualities allowed for in the New Testament Church. This is very relevant from the missionary viewpoint (the possible validity of a eucharistic celebration even without a priest, for example in China or South America), from the ecumenical viewpoint (recognition of the validity of ministries and sacraments in a Church whose presidents do not historically enjoy the special 'apostolic succession'), and even within the Church (assessment of opposition groups).

7. THE NORMATIVE VALUE OF THE EXEGETICAL EVIDENCE

If the tendency to an institutional ministry cannot claim a normative value, change in respect to the origins—change as such—cannot be assessed as degeneration. Our survey has shown that the New Testament recognizes various types of organization and administration of the community; they cannot be reduced to one another, even though they have fused in the course of time. Hence the New Testament does not allow us to 'canonize' any one form of community constitution. No one can justifiably assert that today this would necessarily be wrong for the Church. On the contrary, this gives it the freedom to get in step with the times, to be ready for new developments and a remoulding of ecclesial ministry for the good of man and the community. It is not just a question of searching the New Testament for isolated models which we then try to imitate: instead the New Testament offers determinative elements which have to be maintained and confirmed in quite different circumstances if we are to claim the title of Christians.

As far as the service of leadership in the community is concerned, the following are decisive features in the New Testament. It must be:

(*a*) service to the community;

(*b*) faithful to the norm laid down by Jesus, which will not tolerate any dominative relationship;

(*c*) indebted to the primitive witness of the apostles;

(*d*) operative within a multiplicity of different functions, services and charisms.

Three

DEVELOPMENT OF THE
TRADITIONAL
CONCEPTION OF OFFICE

I. EVIDENCE FROM THE HISTORY OF THE CHURCH

(a) The history of ministries in the Church is unusually complex and varied. In the primitive period, as we have seen, local communities had different forms of organization which only gradually—at first sporadically in Syria with Ignatius of Antioch, then generally from the end of the second century—became conflated in the relatively *unified system* of a monarchical episcopate with presbyters and deacons. Changes also occurred in the structure of ecclesial ministry which extended to developments within the Church—to theological processes, but also to a growing interpretation of Church, State and society. There were many advantages in this process, but they were accompanied by several disadvantages. There had already been a radical break with the pre-Christian and non-Christian priesthood when, mainly at the beginning of the third century, the previously strictly avoided *titles* of 'priest' and 'high priest' (*hiereus, archiereus, sacerdos, summus sacerdos*) came to be used, not (as yet) for presbyters, but for the episcopal ministry, which then began to display a more strongly liturgical emphasis.

Already in the second century, adopting certain Old-Testament and pagan images without any apparent break, the eucharistic celebration had developed in the direction of a properly *sacrificial action*. The structure of ecclesial service was (significantly) adjusted to that of the Roman civil service, with its '*ordines*': services arranged as finely graduated '*offices*'. The bishop became a high functionary administering a territory, with presbyters, deacons and other ministers of the church as his subordinates, while he himself was subject to the metropolitan and the patriarch, who were—respectively—religious leaders of a province or a part of the Empire. Whereas, very early on, he had presided over the liturgical celebrations of the community as a whole, the bishop was now set over the differentiated ministerial functions which, in the various parts of his territory, were exercised by presbyters, deacons and other ministers. Despite the existence of other ecclesial functions, which allowed room for a greater degree of flexibility, the *episcopate*, *presbyterate* and *diaconate* were henceforth considered to be the obligatory ministerial structure, imparted by the laying-on of hands and by prayers; the respective functions of these ministries continued to change signally.

From the fifth and sixth centuries above all, there was a process of full sacralization and ritualization: the service of the word regressed; cultic and ritual activity became that which was proper to the priesthood; liturgical power and the specific sanctity and dignity of the ministry were reified. In the background of this development it is important to note an increasing solemnization of worship, the establishment of a parallel between the ministries of the New Testament and the priesthood of the Old Testament, and unrestricted assimilation of extra-Christian religious customs, a reduction in catechetical instruction and an associated increase in infant baptism, and the inadequate education of priests in politically difficult times. 'The world' still passed for Christian; the communities concentrated on themselves, on their cultic worship and internal discipline. Canon law acquired a central position and, in the Middle Ages, to a large extent ultimately determined sacramental theology, and above all that relating to the sacrament of Orders.

(*b*) The general historical *relativity* of titles, of dress, and of symbols of office, but also of the outward and inward forms of the ministries of leadership, conditioned as they are by numerous economic, cultural, political and psychological factors, is clear and unmistakable. A long road led from the charismatics of Corinth and the elders of Jerusalem to the bishops, presbyters and deacons of the Church of the martyrs, then to the monk-priests, to the clergy of the basilicas, and to the bishops of the court of the Christian Empire; and another long road from the secular priests, canons, court chaplains, prince-bishops and popes of the Middle Ages to the pastors and moderators of the Reformation era, to the directors of consciences, missionaries, worker priests and student chaplains of modern times.

It should be noted that an ecclesiastical *state* or mode of life was a product of the last phase of the Old World and of the early Middle Ages. From the fourth century, special privileges, immunities and titles of honour; from the fifth century, traditional vestments which did not follow secular variations, first in worship and then for ordinary life (though in the Catholic Church, admittedly, a special 'uniform' became obligatory only from the sixteenth century); towards the end of the fifth century the monastic tonsure was adopted, and from the sixth century celibacy became increasingly common; from the eighth century (when Latin was no longer understood by the people) there was a special language, a special form of instruction, a special liturgy (and later the obligation to say a special form of 'priestly' prayers—the breviary).

(c) For a theological, and therefore practical, understanding of ecclesial service, the *sacramental conception* of this ministry, which dates from the Middle Ages (but, in fact, has its origins in patristic times) is significant. With the researches of the high Middle Ages into the concept of a sacrament and with the process of reflection that gradually produced the seven sacraments in the twelfth and thirteenth centuries, it was necessary to define precisely the sacramental nature of ecclesial ordination—a sacramentality concentrated on the presbyterate. The sacramental nature of the presbyterate was considered to be a function of the eucharist, which at that time was conceived primarily as a sacrifice. As a 'priesthood' exercised in the 'sacrifice' of the mass, the presbyterate came to be the central sacramental office, with its own specific sacramental 'character'. The diaconate, now no more than a mere auxiliary service at the mass, lost its specific consistency. Even though the ministerial significance of the episcopate was considerably reduced, from the juridical and pragmatic viewpoint it remained the office with which the central administration of major ecclesiastical territories was associated.

For the Church as a whole, the Gregorian reform and its completion of a development begun in Rome in the fourth and fifth centuries meant that the *papacy* took on its specifically medieval form from the eleventh century (with a peak in the thirteenth and another in the fifteenth century); the juridical form of organization prevailed, and led to a centralized absolutism in the administration of the Church, which brought about a break between the Church in the West and the Churches of the East, which had not evolved in the same way.

(*d*) This short historical survey is intended to bring out, by stressing their relativity, those elements in the development of the traditional 'priesthood' that are obviously of a later date and can never claim the normative value of the origins. As far as anything associated with these later elements is concerned, there is no question of any irreversibility. There can be no decisive objections on such grounds against a new conception and a renewed form of the ministry of leadership in the Church.

2. DECISIONS OF THE MAGISTERIUM

(*a*) At the time of the Reformation, the differing standpoints in the quarrel about a precise understanding of the ministry were marked by polemics on both sides. On the Catholic side, the traditional dogmatic conception of office was fixed in detail by the Council of Trent: so much so that until Vatican II the understanding and structure of ecclesial service were still determined by the Tridentine definitions and anathemas. In opposition to the Reformers, who stressed the universal priesthood, Trent affirmed the existence of a visible priesthood with a full and exclusive power in regard to the sacrifice of the mass and penance, institution by Christ and the sacramental nature of ordination, an indelible sacramental character, and the existence of a hierarchy established on a divine basis and consisting of bishops, priests and deacons. In general the Reformers also held firmly to the divine institution of a service of proclamation and administration of the sacraments, for which a designation was legally requisite. They put the relation of the ministry to the actual community to the fore.

(*b*) Whereas Vatican I, with definitions regarding papal jurisdiction and infallibility, increased the divergence between the Catholic understanding of ministry and the Protestant position, Vatican II created important conditions for a reconciliation. The Council is relevant here above all because (even though from the dogmatic viewpoint it maintained certain traditional structures of ministry) it drew attention to decisive aspects of the New Testament. In the Constitution on the Church those stressed most of all are: (i) the Church is primarily the people of God and the community of the faithful; (ii) accordingly the emphasis is on the nature of service and the collegiality of ecclesial service; (iii) the universal priesthood is strongly insisted upon; (iv) the charismatic dimension of the Church is acknowledged and well brought out; (v) the importance of the local church is recognized.

An important fact is Vatican II's reference to a central canon of the Council of Trent (Sess. XXIII, canon 6; cf. note to No. 28 of the Constitution on the Church: *Lumen gentium*, III). Vatican II makes three corrections to this canon: (i) the Council of Trent used the non-biblical term 'hierarchy', which Vatican II replaces by the expression 'church ministry' (*ministerium ecclesiasticum*); (ii) whereas at Trent '*divina ordinatio*' would seem to have referred, too, to a division of ministries among bishops, presbyters and deacons, at Vatican II '*divinitus institutum*' refers without any possible confusion to the ecclesial ministry as such; (iii) whereas at Trent the hierarchy 'consists' (*constat*) of bishops, presbyters and deacons, for Vatican II the ecclesial ministry is 'exercised' (*exercetur*) by those who, from antiquity (*ab antiquo*, and therefore not from the origins), 'have been called' (*vocantur*) bishops. Similar corrections are made to the end of Chapter II of the Constitution of the Church, when a more precise and detailed definition has to be given of the ministries of bishop, priest and deacon.

(*c*) Even apart from the foregoing, the comparison with Vatican II forces us to ask the following basic, critical questions about Trent:

(i) Is Trent, considered historically (and not merely juridically and canonically), truly representative of the whole Church? What does that entail for the effective authority of the Council?

(ii) Were the Reformers really condemned—or, in fact, understood?

(iii) Was there any pastoral weight to the Tridentine doctrinal decrees?

(iv) Did Trent, in sacramental doctrine and practice, take into account the known historical development of its own time?

(v) Did Trent really take the original Christian message into consideration?

(*d*) These questions point to the historical relativity not only of the actual form taken by the ministry, but of its dogmatic expression. These Tridentine definitions also raise the urgent question of the infallible nature of certain propositions of the Church. Only a basic resolution of the infallibility question will allow us to come closer to resolving the post-Tridentine problems in a way appropriate to the demands of the present age and the claims of the gospel. In any case, nowadays the Tridentine definitions can no longer constitute a decisive obstacle to a renewal of our understanding of, and of the forms of, ecclesiastical ministry. The ecumenical perspectives and possibilities that this finding opens up seem obvious.

3. HISTORICO-THEOLOGICAL NOTES

I add a few exegetical and theological notes to help elucidate the preceding remarks. They are provisional since I intend to present and substantiate them in greater detail in a longer work on the doctrine of the sacraments.

a. *The concept of a sacrament*

(i) It is an analogical concept. Even if one restricts it to cultic actions, it comprises actions that are not perhaps wholly disparate ('equivocal'), that are in any case not purely and simply identical ('univocal'), but instead both, often being more unlike than like (analogous). How much or how little have the installation of a canon and the 'sacramental' of the blessing of salt to do with baptism, and the consecration of a church building with the Lord's Supper? What exactly is there in common between the Lord's Supper and a marriage or the laying-on of hands?

(ii) The sevenfold nature of the seven sacraments is a product of history. Unknown during the first thousand years, presented for the first time in the twelfth century (and initially without any claim to exclusiveness), the seven prevailed in practice. Only three centuries before the Reformation an official church document took up the matter, and subsequent Councils treated it as a matter of faith. Hence the concept of a sacrament proved to be not only analogical but extremely variable, being defined variously in different epochs.

(iii) The traditional seven sacraments are not all on the same level. The New Testament usually derives baptism and the eucharist directly from Jesus Christ; both have from the start played an important part in all church communities. The case of Orders is quite different. What do the Pauline epistles (of unimpeachable authenticity, and the major witnesses for the constitution of the primitive Church) say about ordination? Strictly, nothing. The Acts of the Apostles thirty, and the Pastoral Epistles fifty, years later, mention the ordination of the leaders of communities. Centuries passed before ordination, in line with baptism and the Lord's Supper, was counted among the sacraments. In fact (and in this case the first canon of the decree on the sacraments give a false impression), Trent did not intend all the sacraments to be put on the same level. On the contrary, the decree on the eucharist underlines the pre-eminence of this sacrament over the others. At the same time, in the decree on justification, there is a clear emphasis on the fundamental importance of baptism, the sacrament of faith, for justification. The distinction between major and minor sacraments is to be thought of as a matter of tradition.

(iv) The number of the sacraments depends on how we define a sacrament. At all times, whatever might be designated as a 'sacrament' depended on this definition: in early times the pledge, then the oath of loyalty to the flag or the act of blessing; later, with Christianity—in relation to the Greek '*mysterion*'—the mysteries of the Trinity, the Incarnation, the work of Christ, and specific facts of his life, the meaning of the gospels, or particular cultic actions. The definition decided which of the cultic actions known as sacraments actually deserved the term. Was it only baptism and the Lord's Supper, or ordination, royal anointing, the consecration of nuns, and marriage too? The less the content of a concept is fixed, the greater its extension—this is an old principle of Aristotelian logic—and reciprocally, the more precise the concept of a sacrament, the less sacraments there are: thirty (Hugh of St Victor), twelve (Peter Damian), seven (Peter Lombard, the great schoolmen and Trent), six (pseudo-Dionysius), five (the *Summa sententiarium*, the school of Anselm of Laon and William of Champeaux), four (the early medieval theologians who stressed especially baptism and chrism, the body and blood), three (Isidore of Seville), or two (a broad tradition from the early Fathers down to the Reformers).

(v) Institution by Christ is an open question. If (like Trent) one considers institution by Christ to be an essential 'aspect' of a sacrament, then one has from the start to disallow most of the thirty sacraments of Hugh of St Victor, which would then be 'sacramentals' and not sacraments. But if—as Luther and the Reformers asserted— institution by Christ (understood in the very strict sense of a direct institution explicitly recorded in the New Testament) was the essential 'aspect' of the sacrament, then some of the seven of the high Middle Ages would have to be disallowed. They would no longer be sacraments, but 'Christian customs', or something like that. Trent does not help in elucidating the question, since it took over the medieval definition and with it the seven sacraments, thus disdaining the new, very much biblically and historically oriented standpoint of the Reformers. Trent was not in a position to prove institution by Christ in the strict sense for confirmation, extreme unction, sacramental marriage, or ordination. But (with the aid of a few distinctions) it nevertheless continued to call them sacraments, and to derive grave obligations from this classification. The Protestant solution, which was then illuminating in many ways, is not now straightforwardly acceptable without close scrutiny. In the meantime criticism from Protestant exegetes has shown the fundamental importance of baptism and the eucharist, but has cast doubt on the traditional idea of their institution by Jesus. In short, the question of institution by Jesus, the question of the definition of a sacrament, and that of the number of sacraments, are posed nowadays in a new way and have to be given a new answer—one that takes into account all the recent results of modern exegesis and of the historical study of dogmas. The speculative derivation of the seven sacraments from the Church itself as the 'primordial sacrament' is arbitrary precisely in settling for the number seven; it can only obscure and not resolve these questions. Only a constructive critique of dogmatic adjustments that is devised in the light of a Christian message that is more exactly revealed thanks to exegesis will devote itself more to its real cause than to abstract definitions, and thus be of any effective use.

b. *The sacramental 'character'*

(i) The scriptural texts traditionally quoted in favour of an indelible 'sacramental character' *(character indelebilis)* or seal with which God marks those who believe in him, clearly intend reference to the Holy Spirit himself (in relation, it would seem, to baptism), and not to a spiritual 'sign' distinct from the Holy Spirit, and stamped into the soul (character=mark, stamp). It was the Greek and Latin Fathers of the first centuries who, when speaking of the Holy Spirit, and in certain cases of baptism, used the term 'seal', which clearly concerns not only the soul but the body.

(ii) Augustine—embarrassed by his confrontation with the Donatists, to whom he had to prove that baptism is no more repeatable than ordination, and that baptism given by heretics is valid—'invented' the 'sacramental character'. He used the word 'character' for the first time to designate something distinct from the Holy Spirit (from baptism and ordination) and from the (created) 'grace' bestowed on that occasion, without being able to ground this something on Scripture or on previous tradition. But for Augustine it is a question of an *ad hoc* pragmatic justification without subsequent speculative reflection. The character imprinted in the soul is comparable to the physical marking of a soldier, or to a seal by virtue of which certain rights are bestowed. Later Latin theology took over the idea without verifying the existence of such a character.

(iii) It was only towards the end of the twelfth century and the beginning of the thirteenth that the *doctrine* of the sacramental character underwent methodical development; but its existence was already implicitly accepted in the case of baptism, confirmation and orders. The first application of this doctrine is to be found in a document of the magisterium from Pope Innocent III. After the first Franciscan school and Albert the Great, it was mainly with Thomas Aquinas that the doctrine of an indelible sacramental character was really developed and constructed (the character now being understood as a *potentia*). All the consequences were drawn from the speculative but also from the canonical viewpoint: the character created a permanent juridical bond in regard to the Church, and in particular the character produced by ordination grounded the impossibility of any return of an ordained man to the lay state. However, at the end of the thirteenth century, Scotus criticized the scriptural and traditional proofs of this doctrine, but asserted the existence of a character by referring to the authority of the 'Church'. For Durandus, the character had no real existence, being but a mere rational relation (*relatio rationis*).

(iv) On this point, too, the Council of Trent did not take the Reformers' difficulties seriously, but confirmed without any serious discussion the medieval doctrine and the 'Decree for the Armenians' of the Council of Florence. In this way what was originally only the unpretentious supposition and expedient solution of a great theologian became more than a thousand years later a dogma of the Church, requisite under threat of excommunication. Since then the explanation has been offered that the sacramental character exists actually as an 'accident' of

the soul; more precisely it is a supernatural quality in-
hering physically in the soul; and yet no one has ever
succeeded in proving from Scripture or venerable tradition the existence of this character, distinct from the
spirit, from baptism or confirmation, and the grace bestowed by one or the other.

(v) Present-day Catholic theology has become very
much aware of these difficulties, but, since it is defined as
infallible doctrine, most Catholic theologians have recourse to the habitual ploy of trying to circumvent such
problems by means of a special interpretation of the
'indelible character', even though it was defined quite
clearly by medieval and post-Tridentine theology. The
mark impressed by God now becomes a 'life plan' chosen
by the individual, and the indelible (though invisible!)
sign a sign for the community. The ecclesiological interpretation of 'character' even goes so far as to describe it as
that which constitutes the Church in a visible community of worship and grace: the indestructibility of the
sign grounds the everlasting nature of the Church. But
no speculation which ignores history, and no exaggera-
tion, can prove that there is a something distinct from the
Holy Spirit, baptism or ordination, and from the grace
bestowed.

As for Augustine's intention, which in itself deserves
wholehearted assent, there are better ways of according
with it. The unrepeatable nature of baptism and ordination (like the participation of all in the priesthood of
Christ—which Thomas grounded on the character) can
also be affirmed without recourse to the actual impression
in the soul of this sign. This non-repeatability relies on the
unique and *definitive* character of the beginning that God has
enacted with man in Christ, and which makes a repetition
senseless—all the more so for a sacrament of initiation.
The many difficulties presented by an indelible character
conceived thus are removed merely by recourse to the
original Christian conception for which this 'indelible

seal' is none other than the very gift of the Holy Spirit, into whose service man is taken permanently and in his whole life. A far-reaching critical revision is necessary of the concept of a 'created' grace and a 'state of grace'.

c. *The concept of sacrifice*

(i) The idea of the eucharist as a sacrifice prevailed at an early date and became part of the understanding and practice of past ages without any realization of its alien nature. In the Eastern Churches, the eucharist retained the aspect of a meal, whereas in the West, mainly the interest awakened by the doctrine of sin and grace, and then the legalistic thought of Rome, eventually brought about a concentration on, and finally an emphatic restriction to, the notion of sacrifice. But there was a great divide between the declarations of the Fathers on the sacrificial character of the eucharist and the immensity of the sacrificial imagery of medieval theology, liturgy and piety. The distance was the greater the more these ideas were associated with the theory of satisfaction, votive masses and masses for the dead, the multiplication of clerical orders and sacrificial altars, the repression of active participation in the Lord's Supper (communion once a year under one of the two kinds) in favour of the cult of the host which replaced it (ocular communion, miraculous hosts, the feast of the body of Christ, processions, 'exposition' of the most holy sacrament): all evidence of a religious mentality that prevailed during the post-Tridentine epoch and right up to Vatican II.

(ii) Whereas the great schoolmen were concerned mainly with the question of the real presence, and for them the relation of the sacramental sacrifice to the sacrifice of the Cross became part and parcel of the ancient ideas of representation and *memoria*, after the Tridentine definition of the sacrificial character of the mass there was an immense amount of speculation on the theme of sacrifice, the theories of which need not be related here but—like the Tridentine decisions themselves—require a critique based on the New Testament. It is in this direction that the following exegetical remarks are oriented.

(iii) Throughout the New Testament, the *death of Christ on the Cross* is understood as a sacrifice of expiation for sins. But this sacrifice implies no reconciliatory influence on an angry God. It is not God but man who has to be reconciled: the death of Christ is the end of all the sacrifices by means of which men sought to reconcile themselves with God. And the sacrifice of Christ does not imply the offering of external gifts: Jesus offers himself, and his death is the *end of all those sacrifices* in which man offered expiatory victims. The Epistle to the Hebrews shows clearly that the sacrifice of Jesus, because it is the perfect sacrifice, was offered 'once and for all', and henceforth rendered superfluous other expiatory sacrifices. As for the glorified Lord, he does not offer himself again in sacrifice: he, the Crucified and Glorified, is the eternal High Priest who always stands before God on behalf of his own. Though offering less scope for errors of interpretation than the idea of sacrifice, the idea of representation (also biblical) belongs in this context, and should now be restored to its rightful place.

(iv) Accomplished once and for all, the sacrifice of Jesus exercises its action on the community. And the community is made to share in the sacrifice of Christ *in the Lord's Supper*. Christ enables the community to enter into the new alliance established by the blood of his sacrifice for the multitude. The accounts of the Supper also use sacrificial terminology, but—for the same reason precisely—there is no question of the eucharistic celebration of a renewal or of a completion, still less of an outbidding of this unique sacrifice of expiation. The eucharistic celebration is not itself a sacrifice, but, ever and again, it refers to the unique sacrifice of Christ on the Cross, which through it becomes present and operative. As for the eucharistic offerings, their meaning—their essence—is to attribute the sacrifice of Christ to his own.

(v) By the sacrifice of Christ, the *community* is also called to sacrifice. And from it not only outward offerings are expected, but the total gift of the man himself: these are not material but spiritual sacrifices: of praise of God, of thanks, of faith, of obedience, of love—a sacrifice of praise and thanks consisting of a gift of self not restricted to the cultic assembly but manifested as a daily sacrifice in the everyday world.

(vi) In this way the community does not put a second sacrifice of expiation at the side of the expiatory sacrifice of Jesus; instead it praises and gives thanks for the sacrifice that Jesus made once and for all, and which, by virtue of the eucharistic celebration, it is enabled to share in. The man who presides over this celebration may not be thought of as a *sacrificing priest*. To conceive oneself thus contradicts the New Testament as a whole, and in particular the Epistle to the Hebrews.

I repeat, however: statements made in the restricted framework of the present essay cannot be anything more than very provisional indications allowing a reference to tradition which shows how there is room for a new understanding and a growth of new forms of the ministry of ecclesiastical leadership.

Four

THE FORM OF THE MINISTRY OF LEADERSHIP IN THE CHURCH

I. TYPES OF RELIGIOUS LEADERSHIP

Today it is less easy than ever to make out the essence of ecclesial 'office'. Without doubt, the identity crisis which affects many parish priests, chaplains and even bishops, is primarily the result of the fact that, to tell the truth, no one any longer knows what a 'priest' or bishop is, and *for what reason* he is a 'priest' or bishop. Is he mainly a liturgist, or a preacher, or an organizer? Is his primary task catechesis, or giving practical help? Is his activity directed towards the community, or outwards and towards society?

In the light of the New Testament we have seen that it is a matter of administration, of presiding over the community. From the sociological viewpoint, this concept of community administration—on the local, regional or universal scale—is comprised in the broader conception of the religious leader. There are several ways of being a religious leader; among those actually practised, sociologists of religion have discerned a number of types. According to Joachim Wach, in religions (apart from Shamanism) the most important religious character is the *founder* who founds a (major or minor) tradition, institution or community. Afterwards, the *reformer* introduces new impulses and energies into an existing tradition, institution or community, or even, perhaps, gives it a new direction. On the basis of a direct religious experience, the *prophet*—without any new establishment or planning— speaks with force within the given situation, and the *visionary*, somewhat like the prophet, but addressing himself instead to the surrounding group, gives his interpretation to the disciples. There is also the *magician*, who, apart from the explanations he gives to his fellow men, can obtain specific effects for them; the *soothsayer*, who is capable not so much of attaining certain objectives as of using a 'practical' method to tell his client what can happen to him. Finally the *saint* shows what has definitive value for men, not so much through his knowledge or his craft as *by virtue of what he is*. As the servant of the cult, the *priest* mediates between men and the deity; the *religious* man, by virtue of his special personal position in the community, acts by way of example and exerts unusual authority.

These are charisms, vocations in the widest sense of the term: each of these types has supplied one element or the other for integration in the traditional conception at some time or another—in one case more, in another less. But it is also clear that the service of leadership in the Church, the diverse forms of which are sketched in the New Testament, cannot be purely and simply identified with one or the other of these sociological types. Several of the individuals just mentioned are firmly rejected, even in their modern form, by at least the younger generation of priests. These are, in the context of a certain conception of the sacrament *(opus operatum)*, the rôles of magician and soothsayer, and that of the sacrificing priest as an ordained intermediary marked off from the community. All the more necessary, then, to know what is essential and decisive for the service of leadership in the Church. The message of the New Testament, as briefly indicated in Chapter II, still allows us to see what ought to remain and what ought to be changed, what stays throughout history and what is transformed in its course. To use mathematical language, in this 'function' it is possible to discern 'constants' and 'variables'. Together, both determine the historical existence of the ecclesial ministry in its historical *form*, and reveal both the continuity in discontinuity, and the discontinuity in continuity.

I shall begin with the variables, in order then to be able to indicate the constants more clearly. Then what might seem strong criticism of the traditional conception of office will be shown to be unequivocally in the service of the positive interpretation to be developed directly afterwards. This should help us to see clearly how in the present identity crisis, the parish priest, chaplain or bishop, can understand his ministry and himself. This understanding will not be merely sociological, as if the models in question were drawn from society; it will be resolutely theological, the product of a process of reflective interpretation of the New Testament message itself. What, then, are the variables of something that, to follow the inspiration of the New Testament, might be called the service of administration (the president's ministry, *kybernesis*)?

2. VARIABLES OF THE MINISTRY OF LEADERSHIP

Still too few are aware that the gospel shows how there is a great deal of freedom for the ecclesial community to structure its administrative ministry, and a great deal of scope for answering the varied needs of man today in our society. Not only the principle '*sacramenta propter homines*' but '*ministeria propter homines*' constitutes authority. It will soon be clear that the following viewpoints are partly connected and transposable.

(*a*) The service of administration in the Church is not necessarily a full-time ministry. It is not absolutely necessary that it should be a profession. It would of course be illusory to think that with its high degree of differentiation, our technical society, for example in the case of large parishes or certain functional communities (such as universities or hospitals), could wholly dispense with full-time community leaders. On the contrary, they will always be very necessary. But the possibility of community presidents for whom this service would be a second profession and who would continue to exercise their vocations as workmen, technicians, officials, teachers or physicians (they would have the apostle Paul as their model) is at least as serious as the diaconate re-established by Vatican II. With the additional leisure time that many will benefit from, this 'half-time' ministry could prove very practical for non-territorial communities. It would not be a case of priests becoming workers (worker priests), but of workers making themselves 'priests': new categories of community leader, whose training would not be a general theological culture, but very precisely oriented as well as adapted to the intellectual level of the community in question.

(b) The ministry of leadership in the Church is *not necessarily* a lifelong task. It should not be an obligation for life. It is true enough that the service of the community in the spirit of the gospel will seize a man at another level of his existence than that touched by something different, and for more than one there will be no meaning in it unless it is 'for life'—which should not, of course, be wrongly interpreted in the sense of an 'indelible character'. Even when it is a part-time occupation, the service of leadership in the Church will never be just one 'job' among others. It is a straightforward question of a commitment of faith. However, at least since Vatican II, the retirement of bishops for reason of considerable age has been held out as possible, and even the desire that it should be so has been stated firmly. It is not my task here to examine why the church ministry—whether it is the only profession or much more obviously the second profession—cannot in certain cases really be a lifetime occupation. The seriousness of commitment will not suffer any more than when someone enters a peace corps or works in development aid. A limitation in time can give rise to an even greater intensity of effort.

(c) The ministry of leadership in the Church is not a situation—a social *position*. Admittedly the ministry was for a long time identified with the clerical state. But with Vatican II the Catholic Church itself realized that the habit does not make the monk, and that for the church leadership as well, the time of symbols and class privileges was past. At the same time, not only from a sociological but from a theological viewpoint, there no longer seemed to be any basis for the sacralization that accompanied the assimilation of service in the Church to a social position, and which made the man exercising it a sacred person separate from other men, and exalted above ordinary Christians as an intermediary with God: when ordination would seem more important than baptism. To ground ecclesial service in a 'christological' way, while ignoring the community and isolating its leader from it as a sort of 'second Christ', is contrary to the New Testament concept of a universal priesthood according to which all believers, by faith and baptism, live by the gospel, for the world and for their fellow men. The minister is perfectly right to refuse this kind of sociological separation—with a theological or christological justification. He no longer wishes, for the sake of the interests of bourgeois society, to be taken, from the cradle to the grave, from the blessing of the British Legion flag to the national event, as the priest who consecrates all the family, local and national events that can arise, even when they haven't much to do with Christianity. In present-day democratic society, it is both psychologically understandable and theologically permissible that whoever is in charge of the community should wish to be a Christian among Christians, a *man among men*, so that he may be able on the basis of his faith to confirm his worth as a man in commitment with his fellow humans.

(*d*) The ministry of leadership in the Church does not require a university training; it is not a science. Evidently, at a time when general culture is expanding, when equal educational opportunities are demanded and professional life has increasingly an appropriate academic training, we should not underestimate the importance of the academic education of the community leader. It was not without reason that certain saints of the past preferred a confessor without piety but with enlightenment to a pious though ignorant guide. It is not unusual in pastoral practice for theological ignorance to be a cause of immobility; in this area today there is hardly any risk of knowledge being out of place. At the same time, despite the importance of a university education and of the rôle of 'masters', of theologians, in the Church, the question arises: is the man with a university education the only one who can look after a community? Aren't there communities—whether territorial or functional—which do not necessarily need a university level of education in their leader? A leader whose ecclesial service is his second occupation can surely have another kind of training (for example, that proper to a skilled workman) which would in certain cases balance the lack of university education? Admittedly, in order to discourage a non-enlightened fanaticism (triumphalism or legalism), greater value should be attached to an appropriate training for a community leader. With the present variety of possible preparations (evening courses, weekend courses, training weeks, holiday courses) this should be a practical possibility. As for the theologians responsible for such training courses, they will be faced not with a less exacting but with a more exhausting form of teaching.

(*e*) The office of leadership in the Church does not require *celibacy*, and does not necessarily include renunciation of marriage. In the Catholic Church, any defender of the law of celibacy who deems it both compatible with the freedom of the gospel of Jesus Christ and useful for pastoral purposes, will admit that it is a mere law of the Church that originated in the Middle Ages. In addition a growing number of people among the Catholic laity and clergy believe that (on the basis of the gospel) celibacy can mean only a *freely chosen vocation* (charism) and not a law comprising a general obligation. Leaders who are not married will remain very useful to the Church, in view of tasks which, in mission countries or in their own countries, require a commitment beyond the ordinary (travel, long absence, and so on). Jesus and Paul lived a celibate life of exemplary value in the service of their fellow men. But they expressly left everyone free in this regard. Peter and the other apostles were married—while carrying out their church ministries. For many centuries this seemed obviously acceptable for community presidents, bishops and presbyters, and has been retained in the East, even in the Eastern Churches united with Rome, at least for the presbyters—with quite negative effects in the case of the (illogically though obligatorily) unmarried bishops. Monastic communities, the law of celibacy (in a sort of pan-monasticism) was extended to all the secular clergy in the course of the high Middle Ages; radically put in question at the time of the Reformation and again nowadays, celibacy is not only repugnant to the liberal rule of the primitive Church but to the present understanding of individual liberty and the rights of man.

Maintained today by recourse to all the means of clerical authoritarianism and to pseudo-theological arguments, the tradition proper to the Latin Church would ignore the fact that throughout all the epochs of the Church's history, from the first to the twentieth century, there have been married Catholic presbyters who have looked to their ministry, and often in an exemplary fashion. Therefore, through the blindness and inflexibility of the church authorities, the law of celibacy has become, for many priests and chaplains, the test-case for a renewal of the ecclesiastical ministry and 'system'. The resignations from the ministry, which are immense in number (from twenty-two to twenty-five thousand priests, chaplains and even bishops in the last eight years), and in many countries the lack of recruits, which is already catastrophic (for all Holland, where in 1959 there were still about four hundred ordinations a year, there were only four ordinations of secular priests in 1970), make a change requisite, which in many respects will come too late and not be without considerable losses. The present pope and epis-copate will be responsible before the history of the Church for a development which was foreseeable for a long time. The appropriate solution will not be provided by illogical half-measures, such as the admission of married (and therefore older) men, but only by the restoration of primitive Christian freedom, which church leaders them-selves have no right to reduce. My account serves to show that in the crisis of the church ministry there is much more in question than a celibacy crisis, but at the same time it shows that this crisis of the ministry is most ob-vious in the celibacy crisis, where for individuals it often proves most injurious.

(f) The ecclesial ministry should not be exclusively *masculine*: it should not be a male league. An equitable re-newal of the Church will include the full participation of women in the life of the Church, on a basis of equal rights. This implies not only that women should exercise re-sponsibility in various deliberative and decision-making bodies (in the Catholic Church, from the parish council to the very devoutly to be wished for 'senate' of the laity of the whole Church), but their admission to special services in the Church and to ordination. We should speak even less of a women's 'priesthood' ('priestesses') than of a male 'priesthood'; however, a number of socio-cultural arguments but no decisive theological objections have been brought against the ordination of women to territorial administrative services and perhaps, above all, non-territorial ones. In this respect the New Testament should be viewed as a time-conditioned work (remember the veiled women of Corinth), and it should be inter-preted on the basis of what I have already said is, in Paul's sense, the 'abolition' of discrimination between men and women. The New Testament communities were already in advance of their time in their valuation of women. Our communities limp behind our own times. From the social and psychological viewpoints, inhibitions and objections against a full equality of rights for women can be overcome in time, as experience in the political sphere shows.

3. CONSTANTS OF THE MINISTRY OF LEADERSHIP

On the basis of the crisis of the ministry of leadership in the Church, and of its origin and history, the preceding points serve to confirm its variability. My delineation of 'constants' will to some extent proceed from the outside inwards: a general framework will be gradually sketched in on our way to the centre.

(a) Essentially, the ministry of leadership in the Church does not intend a form of domination but a service to the community: a permanent service in the Christian community in the sense of a spiritual orientation. The New Testament and the requirements of present-day democratic society demand that this ministry should have a functional basis. This function is not understood here to be primarily sacramental, like that of the consecrator, but primarily ecclesial and social, whatever may still be said of the function of the president in the sacramental action. There should be no confusion between this ecclesiological and functional way of grounding the ecclesial service of leadership and the situationalist misconception which would have it intervene only according to each individual case, and allow it only an occasional function. But there must also be no confusion with the ontological interpretation which postulates an infused ontological quality (a grace of position) as a support for the ecclesial ministry. In the case of the ministry of leadership in the Church we are concerned with a permanent function (even though it might well be part-time); this function is one dependent on a vocation (charism) which affects the individual in a real and lasting way.

(b) The administrative ministry in the Church claims essentially not to be an autocratic form of management which would like to absorb the other functions; it is placed among a multiplicity of diverse functions and charisms; its task is to stimulate, co-ordinate and integrate; it serves the communities and the other ministries, whether those are permanent (catechists, administrators, social workers, various help services, and theologians), or not (visitors' groups, individuals, and so on). In the specialized century in which we live, such a perspective enables us to avoid any irresponsibility arising from a multiplicity of abilities, and allows for the possibility of a new differentiation of functions. It is not necessary that the president or the community leader should be at the same time a wise theologian, and a counsellor who has had a psychological training, and an expert financier, and a teacher . . . (functions that are not, anyway, associated with a presbyteral ordination: in the Eastern Churches, for example, the theologians are today still mostly laymen as in the first years of the Church). There is no aspect of a university, however good it may be, which could prepare anyone adequately for all functions at once. There are no natural gifts, however exceptional they may be. There is no individual set of abilities that in these days of increasingly specialized requirements, could possibly bear them all, since they always make specialized demands. Now and again, several functions may be united in one individual, and the situation is not always avoidable in actuality; but in principle an accumulation of functions is to be avoided.

How to prevent it is important. The stressed diversity and necessary specialization of these functions mean that there is a very pressing need for the community to aspire to an awakening of different charisms, a common and concerted operation of different vocations, and the co-ordination and integration of different functions on various levels (local, regional, national and international).

Accordingly, the special nature of the ministry of leadership would consist in serving the community and in continuing the specific service of the apostle, which is one of foundation and administration in the Church. Evidently this is not an obvious task that just anyone could fulfil. One has to have the right gifts and aptitudes for the job; one has to have experience of group management and co-ordination; a certain training, even if a scientific training (though very often useful) is not indispensable. There are various forms of leadership in actuality. But the basis remains the charism of leadership: the special vocation to this service of leadership, in the formal sense.

(*c*) The service of leadership in the Church claims essentially not to be a rigid and uniform system of offices, but a service among others, and one which is itself diversified: flexible, mobile, and pluriform according to time and place. Communities are different, as are their structures and possibly also those in charge of them. Large urban parishes may operate as a number of local communities; and, inversely, in the country several village parishes may join together in a regional community. There are territorial communities (parishes) and functional communities (a university community, one in a hospital, a business firm, a tourist resort, a minority language group), communities of the 'service station' kind (with offices at suitable points in a city), or of the 'effective community' variety (designed for a specific form of commitment), and communities of the Catholic, Orthodox and one or another Protestant traditions (with growing integration and a desire for reciprocal recognition in the near future).

We require pluriform communities, which make a pluriform leadership necessary: often, by the nature of things, individual leadership (a one-man operation), but frequently a team or collegiality at work, excludes any undignified and unworthy form of dependence, such as often exists between a curate and a parish priest. But within an administrative ministry there is still room for specialization according to abilities, preferences and training. Instead of a monocracy, teamwork; instead of uniformity, a multiplicity of forms and collegiality.

(*d*) The service of leadership in the Church claims essentially not to be a service at the arbitrary disposition of men; it must be thought of as fulfilling the commission of the Lord of the community, and as a free gift of the Spirit. This service depends on a call, of which the community must be assured: a call from God in the Spirit of Jesus Christ. This vocation, in an inward drive, in the awareness of being fitted for and impelled towards it, is expressed in actual service. The community and those who administer it (possibly also on the higher regional level) may have their part in the actual vocation of a man in church service. But no form of ecclesial administration can make a man without a call into one who is called. A bishop can never replace the Spirit of Christ by merely laying on his hands, if the Spirit is absent; he can never simply commission for the work of leadership those who happen to suit him and who do what he wants. When all human calls have been heard, if the call of God is missing, despite all ordination ceremonies the shepherd will prove to be a hireling. And perhaps it is true to say that unfaithful pastors are as common as false prophets and teachers of lies.

In the Church of Christ, every service of leadership, whether institutionalized or not by the imposition of hands, presupposes a link with the first witness and first mission of the apostles. It presupposes succession in the faith and creed, service and apostolic life. But here there is an even more fundamental implication: in the Church of Christ all leadership presupposes the mandate of the Lord of the community, to the demands of whose gospel and to whose succession those entrusted with the service of leadership—the highest as the servants of all—are bound in a very special way. In the Church of Christ, every

ministry of leadership—with or without ordination—
presupposes most profoundly the call of God's Spirit, of
the Spirit of Christ who bloweth where he listeth and calls
whomsoever he wants; and whose willing instruments
must be both those who send and those who are sent.

Hence the service of leadership, too, is a charism, and
expressly so in Paul's strict sense: a call from God in the
Spirit to a specific service for the community. Of course it
is not enough to claim a charism: a call from God which
impels one inwardly to carry out this service. Anyone
who thinks he hears this call within himself must satisfy a
certain requirement: his vocation must be tested. Try the
spirits! This advice was given to the whole community,
but above all to those in charge of it. The body of the faithful, who have all received the Spirit and who all share in
the special gift of discerning the spirits, should undertake
this examination for each of the presidential services—
whether ordination is in question or not—before ordination, but also and always repeatedly after ordination. Is it
from God, or not? Does he or does he not accord with
what the community needs? In this sense, there is not only
a divine mission but, in a secondary sense, the mission
conferred by the community and those who preside over
it, those who must direct themselves in personal self-
examination in accordance with the basic call from God.

4. CHARISM AND INSTITUTION

(a) The foregoing has emphasized the fact that ecclesial
service is essentially vocation—charism in the strictest
sense. But charism and institution are not obviously identical. It would be a pseudo-solution to the problem to
qualify purely and simply as charismatic the institutionalized ministry (the so-called 'office') and then to refer any
charism directly or indirectly to the institution, integrating it with and subordinating it to the institution. On the
contrary, it must be affirmed that charism in the strict

sense of a call from God in the Spirit of Jesus Christ exists intrinsically and does not derive from the institution. It is a free vocation to a free service in the Church, a vocation that the ecclesial administration can neither cancel nor extend without injury to itself.

A basic direct or indirect 'officialization' of charism is contrary to the New Testament. *A priori*, the charism has no need to be legitimated by an ecclesial institution, as the New Testament shows. On the other hand, there are institutions, and representatives of institutions, who are without anything charismatic: for example, ecclesiastical functionaries who have been ordained, and who exercise their ministry mechanically, showing no trace of any genuine vocation or of the Spirit of Christ. Where the human qualities of leadership are lacking; where there is no ability for dialogue, communication, organization; where human knowledge, initiative, imagination and a will to lead are absent; and where there is no trace of the liberating Spirit of Christ, despite all institutional claims, there is no genuine ministry and no true leadership. The man who has these gifts and uses them, on the other hand, is performing genuine service and leading, even when he possesses no institutional commission. Therefore a charism can be vitally effective without the institution; the Spirit bloweth where he listeth. The institution without charism is dead; only where there is Spirit is there life. Between charism and institution there is always a certain tension, which is never completely absent from someone responsible for a ministry of service. The conclusion to be drawn from all this is that *a distinction has to be made between charism and institution.*

(*b*) But this last assertion includes a second one: charism and institution are not *a priori* inimical: but refer to one another. Conflicts are always possible and often fruitful. The institutionalized ministry needs charism if it is not to be a 'service' without a soul, content to transmit and to administer in the bare sense. Conversely, the institution may be of great help to a charism if it is really aware of being in the service of charisms, of their diversity and vitality; if it detects abilities in the service of the community, co-ordinates them, and eventually re-establishes order among them, and thus serves the cause of the unity and peace of the community.

5. ORDINATION

(a) Ordination has to be seen in the context of charism and institution. For obvious reasons, ordination prevailed in all communities in the *post*-apostolic age, and should be viewed as a wholly *legitimate development* and not as an instance of degeneration. However, one cannot assert that ordination ('ordination to the priesthood') was 'instituted by Christ', since everyone knows that it is neither mentioned nor implicit in any Pauline text. There is not the least proof for this institution. Instead it was taken over from Judaism, as were the colleges of 'elders': the doctors of the Jewish Law, referring to the great Mosaic model, publicly initiated their disciples in the guardianship of the rights and duties of the rabbi. Certain texts on the Pastoral Epistles (and indirectly the Acts of the Apostles) subsequently attributed the ordination of presidents of communities (presbyters, episcopes) to the authority of the apostle Paul. But if today, even in the Catholic Church, ordination is not to fall into ever deeper discredit (which would be an evil), we have to ask: what is its real meaning?

(b) Certainly ordination today can no longer (as in the Middle Ages) pass as a sacral investiture, by virtue of which the receiver is both invested with a kind of universal ecclesial competence in all the appropriate functions, and existentially marked with a 'character' which distinguishes him from the laity: a legal and sacral *'potestas'* that would enable and authorize him alone to consecrate the eucharist, administer the other sacra-

ments, and require, as if in the place of God, an unconditional obedience from inferior clergy. In small details and on a large scale, the time for this divine right has gone, and that which is now specific to the service of leadership in the Church is reduced to the power of pronouncing the words of consecration: in fact, that may offer a kind of global superiority in relation to other faithful, but there is no longer anything in that that would induce a gifted young man to enter into the ecclesial ministry.

We cannot do without a really radical rethinking of the question of ordination. If exegetical research shows objectively that there are in principle other means of access to the services of leadership which are not *a priori* impracticable in our times, that would not mean that ordination even today—on condition of an adapted rite—could not be the most adequate means, an extremely logical means, of access to these services in the Church. Anyone who at the moment of ordination had a more medieval than scriptural conception of it, doesn't need to panic. Consideration of the *primitive* meaning of ordination—which was not wholly lost in the Middle Ages—gives us the chance today to deepen our understanding of it through critical knowledge, instead of watching its disappearance or offering a contorted defence of it. In this way the assent that was given once to ordination will not be lessened but improved, and will stand up to the test of practice.

(*c*) Ordination still has meaning today, if understood in terms of its original meaning. A number of aspects are important: (i) ordination represents a call to the service of leadership, addressed publicly to a believer, by means of which the Church sanctions the call from God; (ii) it is realized in the laying-on of hands and a prayer of intercession; (iii) it gives effect to a spiritual legitimation for the community and for the ordained believer; (iv) all this means that it is the sign of a special apostolic succession of ministries of leadership.

(i) The call issued by men (the Church or those in

charge of the Church) is a public acknowledgment and sanction of a previous call by *God*. In the early Church, ordination was given directly for a specific community, *(ordinatio relativa)*. In view of the nature of the Church, a universally valid ordination *(ordinatio absoluta)* can hardly be excluded. To make the characteristics proper to ordination stand out clearly, we have to use precise distinctions. As an ecclesial vocation, ordination *(ordinatio)*, is not only a call to a specific community (vocation), if possible by virtue of a regular (rite) choice *(electio)*. It is not to be confused with the designation *(nominatio)* given by the church administration for a specific community, nor with induction into a community *(installatio*, investiture), which is a matter of bureaucracy and liturgy. What ordination really is, on the contrary, is the general call to ecclesial service, addressed by the leadership of the Church (if possible with the participation of the ecclesial community), a call which precedes the actual *choice* made by a given community; as the *call* or *designation* for a specific, and 'installation' in a given, community.

(ii) Ordination is a truly spiritual event, in which the Spirit is invoked. It occurs during a prayer of intercession. At the same time, the laying-on of hands is the visible sign of the free gift that is the call of the Spirit, and of the grace of God called down upon one who is to be entrusted with a ministry. The fact that this event is called a 'sacrament' (as has been usual since the high Middle Ages) is secondary in comparison with its spiritual value, and something which depends on the more or less extensive nature of the concept of sacrament applied. If 'institution by Christ' has to derive from the New Testament, then ordination cannot be called a sacrament. However, by the spiritual event of ordination, a man is made accountable for his faith and, with it, his whole existence; he is affected in his being and not only in the action that he carries out. This is true of ordination, whether ecclesial ministry is to be the sole profession, or a second occupation; whether believers undertake it for life or for a short period; whether they are men or women, married or unmarried. In order to express this permanent effect of ordination on one's whole existence, there is no need to have recourse to the doubtful concept of 'official or situational grace', nor to the baseless notion of a sacramental 'character'. In a way that is more obviously convincing for a modern man, a theology of church leadership and service with a New Testament orientation should be able to show where the free call of God's grace, which is the absolute and permanent starting-point for the Church's call, is not just words but an event touching and transforming man in the actuality of his very being.

(iii) Ordination does not take away the humanity and frailty of the individual who receives it. Once ordained, the community leader is still a man subject to sin and error. The efficacy of the service of leadership for the *members of the community* cannot be made to depend on the subjective sanctity of the individual entrusted with it, which is always uncertain and, in the last resort, not open to verification. The one who bestows the grace in each case is not the man in charge of the community but God himself in Christ: Augustine's statement is still valid: 'It is Christ who baptizes.'

But even though ordination does not cancel human frailty, it does equip a man for service and is a plea that the Spirit may come down upon him, and legitimate him as president before a *community* that does not yet know him, since by virtue of his ordination he is officially commissioned to perform this service of leadership in the Church. Hence in this community there is no need to give proof of his charism before being accepted. Because of his ordination, his charism may initially be taken as understood, even though afterwards he must continually show forth the presence of the Spirit and his power. As far as the man who is actually ordained is concerned, if he takes his mission to heart, ordination can give him the assurance that he is truly called and designated as the leader of the community; it can give him the confidence to match his vocation, the courage constantly to tackle the task anew, the trust that, despite all difficulties, doubts and temptations, enables him to persevere to the end in the power of the Spirit.

(iv) Of course ordination is not sufficient in itself to constitute the special 'apostolic succession' of ministries of leadership. But it is certainly a sign of this special apostolic succession of services. It expresses the continuity of the apostolic ministry of leadership and, so long as it is not understood in an exclusive or automatic fashion, it is also effective in helping to stabilize order and leadership in the Church. Yet this apostolic succession would be misunderstood were it restricted to the episcopate.

(d) Intentionally, in this section on ordination I have not mentioned any distinction between the *ordination of bishops and that of priests*. The New Testament evidence shows that the delimitation and articulation of ministries of leadership was a matter of actual development and pastoral adaptation. There is absolutely no reason to make a dogmatic, theological distinction between the ordination of bishops and the ordination of priests. Presbyters and episcopes did not originally constitute two degrees. When the Church began, the ministry of leadership differed according to the community, but was not at all monarchical: it was collegial. After a certain process of uniformity (as my exegetical inquiry has shown), it again took different forms in different Churches. In the Catholic Church, since the time of Ignatius of Antioch, in fact, when community services were expressed in the three degrees of deacons, priests and bishops, the threefold organization of priest, bishop and pope has prevailed. I need not mention the present efforts to re-introduce the diaconate, which had lost its specific value to the extent of becoming no more than a liturgical step to the priesthood. In the Reformation Churches, by a return to the conditions of the ancient Church, the parish priest was treated as a bishop, but without any opposition in principle to a more extensive form of organization; in fact the Reformation Churches also have supra-regional ministries of leadership (bishops, general administrators, presidents of Churches, moderators).

(e) In the matter of ordination for services other than that of leadership, it is certainly possible in principle that someone should be ordained who performs a permanent service in the community (catechists, those in charge of charity schemes, managers, sacristans, and so on). But under the present conditions this seems neither necessary nor desirable. From the primitive period, not all the ministers of the Church but essentially the holders of ministries of establishment and administration, and their assistants, were ordained (hence the so-called minor orders, which degenerated to the condition of temporary liturgical stages on the way to the priesthood, and need not be renewed). Ordination for other ministries could easily come to be a new form of clericalism: i.e., one which would see in other services only an 'extension of administrative services', as was the case for some time with 'Catholic Action'—long thought of as participation in the hierarchical apostolate. Anyway, would all those who had to be ordained willingly accept ordination? It is doubtful, and whatever the case may be in this regard, it is important not to give the impression that charism has no value and cannot last without ministerial or even liturgical acknowledgment. Even this kind of inflation could be abused by the church administration as an additional means of extending uniformity and discipline. It is more important that the other permanent ministries should be not ordained but appropriately and effectively represented in the various organs of decision in the Church.

As far as the rite of ordination is concerned, if it is not to be increasingly opposed, a reform is urgently needed which is appropriate to the present state of theological knowledge. The mission to which the ordinand is referred should be expressed in the liturgy in a clear manner and without any false emphasis. Whereas the Catholic rite suffers mainly from the restriction to a commission to 'offer the sacrifice of the mass', Protestant ordination rites very often suffer from other difficulties, such as commitment to fixed, written and polemically oriented confessions of faith inherited from the Reformation, from an unthinking promise of obedience to church authorities, to the abstract image of a pastor without any other pursuit for the whole of his life.

6. MANDATE FROM THE COMMUNITY AND ITS LEADERS

Because of the charismatic structure of the Church as defined above, there is on all levels (local, regional and universal) a dialectical relation between the community and the service of leadership in regard to the origin of *commission*.

The mandate of the community, as a community in freedom, equality and fraternity, cannot be deduced purely and simply from the ministry of leadership. That would in fact involve a form of clericalization repugnant to Scripture; and the ministry of leadership would be isolated from the community and would become absolutized in regard to succession. But the mandate of the ministry of leadership cannot be deduced simply from the fact that the members form the mandate of the community; from, that is, the universal priesthood. It does not simply derive from the fact that the members of the community, considered individually, delegate their sovereign power; it is not merely the sum, the fusion and the reflection on one man of the sovereign power of all. That would be an inadequate democratization of the community which, at the expense of the same community, would carry out a process of approximation of the level of the ministry of leadership to that of the community.

There has to be a simultaneous solidarity and distinction between the ministry of leadership and the community with all its capacities and particular ministries: in fact, *all* commissions in the Church derive, as has been said, from the Lord, from his Spirit, and remain directly connected to him. Reference to the New Testament will show that this applies to the community and to each Christian. But it also applies to whoever is in charge of the community in terms of his vocation, his special function. He, too, can call on the Lord and present himself before the community in place of Christ as soon as he has the gospel of Jesus Christ effectively behind him. Hence he is not to preach what the community is willing to hear (and of course not just that which it is unwilling to hear), but what the Lord, in a given situation, asks of him and of this community. It is precisely when the community leader is really in the Lord's service that he is really in the community's service too. Then it can be seen clearly that he is acting selflessly, that he is there as a president of the community, and that the community is not there for the president. For this reason, and expressly in the service of the gospel, the president of the community will spare no pains in his effort to realize the needs, difficulties and hopes of his community.

If one really wants to give the community and its president their respective importance, one has to distinguish between the *common mandate* given to every Christian by virtue of the universal priesthood and the mandate of the man put in charge of the community, conferred on him specially by virtue of a special vocation to the official service of the community as such.

7. THE AUTHORITY OF SERVICE IN DEMOCRATIC STRUCTURES

(a) As it derives from the sovereign mandate, the special *authority* of the president of the community within the community is not open to a simple juridical explanation, which would see it as the transmission of a '*potestas*' understood in the Roman sense. The concept of '*potestas ecclesiastica*' (power of the Church in a juridical sense), like its division into two powers, requires a critical theological examination: the power of consecration (*potestas ordinis*=the power of order) and pastoral power (*potestas jurisdictionis*= power of jurisdiction); or into three (if one adds the teaching power). From the theological viewpoint, the special authority of the community leader derives from the special service for which he has been called and has his mandate, whatever the manner in which that may have occurred (election or nomination). The supreme *norm* for the exercise of authority in the Church of Christ is the New Testament message seen in the ever-new perspective of the individual and social situation. If in a particular case the minister certainly has not fulfilled his service according to that norm, he cannot expect submission but on the contrary criticism, and in very serious cases resistance. A blind obedience is incompatible with the dignity and liberty of the reasonable man, of the Christian. A blind obedience can lead to crime, as the recent past has most emphatically shown.

God alone can expect an unconditional obedience; ecclesial authority can never expect it to be more than conditional, if it is itself to correspond in its prescriptions to the will of God expressed in the Christian message.

Therefore church authority is in all respects an authority of service: service to the Lord and to his message, and at the same time service to the faithful and their community. Such an authority, however conditional it may be, is true and effective. The only ones who would wish to see the authority of the president of the community weakened are those who desire the weakening of the community itself. True and effective, this authority is so as a fraternal authority exercised not by constraint like a secular force or power, but as a power enlivened by the Spirit, who prays, exhorts, warns, inspires, asks and convinces. A fraternal authority does not lead men to dependence in a relation of dominance of men over men, but to freedom and love, found in a common obedience of *all* to the one Lord and his gospel. It leads to a reciprocal subordination and, on both sides, to a relative independence of the community and of the community leader: a relative independence varying according to the situation and the circumstances. Jesus and then Paul lived it and showed that this great form of authority is possible: an authority which joins sovereign power and service, yet is not domination but an authority of liberty, and an incentive to freedom.

(*b*) In the present situation, it is in *democratic structures* that the authority of this ministry will see the possibilities and opportunities of realizing the reciprocal service of all required by the New Testament, and the collaboration in a team spirit of the community and those in charge of it in a new democratic society; this will mean on the one hand a return to its own models, and to its original impulsions. But what about actual practice?

(i) *The collegial responsibility of all members of the Church.* The solicitude and work in common asked for nowadays on all levels—for the local, regional and universal Church—require an appropriate degree of common discussion and common decision-making, whether directly or, for reasons of opportunity, by elected representatives supplied with extended rights. Between the person or persons responsible for the community and the elected body, there should be a close and trusting co-operation which will safeguard the rights of the community and those of the leaders of the community (the latter are important lest the various forces in question cancel one another out), or even preserve them by means of a right of veto for both sides in certain specific cases. The obligation to co-operate, which is in many cases a useful suasion to do so—the system of 'checks and balances' in the American constitution—must take a specific form that will obviate any inability and guarantee maximum initiative and progress (the foundation, on a superior level, of an arbitration court for cases of serious litigation). It is also necessary in practice that the exercise of power, which is inevitable even in the Church, should be considered as responsible to the New Testament message and to the needs of the community and society. Then this power would be both legitimated and subject to control.

(ii) *Election of church leaders* by the community in question or (on a higher level: bishop, etc.) by its representatives. The above-mentioned collegial organs of decision could co-operate in this. In this way, as otherwise in cases of collegial responsibility of members of the Church, the tradition of the primitive Church would be restored: this done, one would also have to restore confirmation and control by superior administrative ministries that were then customary. Such an election—from parish priest to pope—should be valid for a longer period, but with a clearly fixed term and an obligatory age limit. In the case where a community demands the retirement of a leader, it is only with the assent of the superior authority, in order to prevent unjust attempts to bring pressure, that such a request should take legal effect.

(iii) *The public character of the Church.* It is also necessary to reach such a degree of clarity and openness in the Church that all the members of the Church can—eventually, at least—have an idea of the important activities of the Church and its leaders. Since financial and pastoral decisions are closely connected, it is not just as a last resort that the budget and the report on the use of church funds, on the local, regional and universal levels, should be offered for universal inspection. In all important matters, information and communication should flow not merely from above downwards, but upwards.

A multiplicity of opinions, criticism and opposition have their legitimate place and require a constant dialogue and the constructive display of contrary ideas. In all this the private sphere of every member of the Church should be respected, just as the various minority groups are to be respected (whether they are *avant-garde* or conservative in nature). In 'matters of faith and morals' nothing can be attained with mere votes. In this regard, where it is impossible to obtain some sort of consensus (not unanimity), it is better to leave the question open according to ancient conciliar tradition.

(iv) *The relative independence of communities*. Since local communities are not only parts of the Church but themselves Churches (manifestations of the one Church), they have a right to autonomy, and similarly, regional and national Churches have a right to autonomy in respect to the universal Church. In the Church, whatever each individual can do with his own power should not be done by the community: whatever the subordinate community and authority do not do, the supreme community has no need to do. The behaviour of the community in regard to the individual, and that of the superior community in regard to the subordinate community, is subsidiary. This is the meaning of the principle of subsidiarity, which allows as much liberty as possible and as much association as necessary. But this implies, too, that no community has the right to shut itself off like a sect. Its autonomy is not absolute, but in many ways relative, inasmuch as subsidiarity carries with it an obligation to solidarity, to a solidarity with other communities, with the regional Church and the universal Church. A community which truly 'serves' will be wholly prepared to co-operate, and even to surrender certain competencies when the good of a community and the general good require it.

8. THE FUNCTIONS OF THE COMMUNITY LEADER

(a) After the immediately foregoing remarks, the reader might well ask what in fact is left of the specific function of the community leader if the community is to be taken into account thus, and allowed to participate in its own running.

Keeping as a basis the 'constants' which originate in the New Testament message itself, despite all 'variables', the ministry of ecclesial leadership may be delimited as follows: the community leader, whatever sort of community he may be charged with, by virtue of a personal vocation which has been publicly examined, permanently leads in the spirit of the Christian message the community, which always shares the responsibility with him. It is a service among other services, differing according to time and place; he performs this service by stimulating, co-ordinating and integrating the various abilities and functions of his community.

This is a general and still too abstract definition of church ministry. What is the substance behind it? To lead the community is, by and large, to see to the 'edification of the community', in the full sense of the term in the New Testament. Nothing would be more false than to view the leader of a community as a kind of functionary, bureaucrat, or managing director, even though very often, in present-day society and the present-day Church, office and managerial work do have something to do with the ecclesial ministry of leadership. But those are mere auxiliary functions, which make the question still more acute: what today are the determinative functions by which the community is administered, led and taught? I have already tried to indicate them; their fundamental rôle in the Church is such that their main lines should be drawn before more detailed adjacent questions are raised. When these functions are in question—particularly in the case of an administrative 'team'—there are many variants and emphases may be placed quite differently. What then are the *basic functions* of the community leader?

(*b*) The direction of a Christian Church or community takes place mainly in the service of the word. In principle, all Christians are used to the proclamation of the word, to the witness of the faith in the Church and the world, to the mission; used too, in urgent cases, to saying for their brothers the words of the remission of sins; but the man in charge of the community, by virtue of his vocation, is— in a no less permanent and public fashion—the one responsible for preaching in the Church and in the world, and in particular for the sermon to the assembled community, and for communal or individual absolution at services of penance. A community that does not assemble is no community; the *Ecclesia* is essentially an assembly. But the call which brings together this assembly is the Christian message, the gospel. Not just any word or action, but the proclamation of the Christian message is decisive in bringing together, constituting and instructing the Church ever anew. It is that proclamation which constantly sends the Church forth into the everyday life of the world. Hence the Church remains the 'work of the Spirit'. That it remains so is the public responsibility of the community leader, a responsibility that, of course, he shares with all, both inwardly and outwardly.

In preaching in all its diverse forms, the president of the community serves the Church which is, despite all differences, and by virtue of the word, a community of faith and the profession of that faith. His preaching is decisive in the orientation of the Church; he prompts and he suggests. In the most various situations he returns to the major questions: where do man and the world come from? where are they going? why? and to what purpose? Perhaps he will pose the true questions more often than he will supply all the answers. He addresses the community in this way, searching among those who are in search of something; a fisher among fishers. At the same time, and always anew, his help brings the individual and society the light of the message of joy and freedom in the midst of the misfortunes and hopes of the moment. And, in the power of the gospel, despite all his weaknesses, he is always capable of renewed comfort and consolation; of reviving, freeing, making happy and, for various reasons, prompting a commitment to action. For the community leader, preaching in the broadest sense of the word should be basic, as service to the gospel and therefore to men. Only in this way will he be able to avoid the risk of sinking to the level of a church functionary.

(c) The leadership of a Christian community or Church is also exercised—just as much as in the service of the word—in the service of *sacraments*. In principle all Christians are empowered to administer baptism and the eucharist; by virtue of his special vocation, the leader of the community has the permanent and public responsibility of ensuring that by baptism—a sign of choice by God and of belonging to the faith—new members are received into the community; he also bears the responsibility of ensuring that by the eucharistic celebration the community constantly gathers together in the most fervent way possible, in thankful memory and praise of the Lord.

If the Church owes it primarily to baptism that the Church *exists*, that it is not the result of its own pious efforts, the eucharist is the sign that despite all decay and error the Church *remains* the Church. If baptism seems above all the sign of the divine grace of choice and justification, and the sign of a responsive faith, the eucharist is the sign of the divine grace which preserves and accomplishes, and the sign of responsive love and hope. In the eucharistic celebration—communion with the Lord or of brothers with one another—the Church and various forms of divine worship find their centre. In the community of the table, at the meal of the action of grace and covenant where, in memory of its Lord, it looks back, raises its eyes, and looks ahead, the community is truly at home, because it is truly at home with its Lord. Hence the visible sign confirms the word and, in the common meal, the unity of the community is made visible as it forms one body. That it should be and remain so, despite all tensions, all differences, all inequalities, is the public responsibility of the community leader—but, here again, all share the same responsibility with him.

In administering the sacraments in their various forms, the president of the co munity serves the unity of this Church to which baptism is an introduction and which the eucharist, the community of love, constantly realizes and manifests. Unity among men requires constant unification.

Relying on proclamation, the president also directs the Church by means of the sacraments. He welcomes into the community, assembles it for the eucharistic celebration and presides over it. He is before all else the man who proclaims the word of God, but he is also the man who speaks in the name of the community before God. All, whatever their differences of class, race or sex, are brought together by him; and, by divine worship, he helps to ensure that men in our consumption and production society, in the fever of this age, do not forget God, and do not vegetate thoughtlessly on the peripheries of their selves. He ensures, on the contrary, that they have time for God, time for the action of grace, praise and prayer, and hence for themselves too; so that, in total confidence in God, they may resist a life that excludes all trust or gives too much of it to another. Subordinate to the service of the word, this service of the sacraments should also be fundamental as a service to the gospel and therefore to men. Only in this way does the leader of the community escape the risk of being no more than a kind of general secretary.

(*d*) Christian logic demands that the leadership of a community or a Church should occur in the service of *committed love*. Even if all Christians are called on to exercise their faith by the exercise of charity, the community leader is specially charged in terms of his own vocation with a permanent, official care that the life of the community should take place in due freedom, and that the faithful, despite all inadequacies, should form a society of committed love among themselves and in regard to the world. I have already stated what this implies for the eliciting and co-ordination of charisms, how the authority of freedom is to be exercised for the freedom of others, and finally how the Church should be a community in liberty, equality and fraternity. The great responsibility of the president of the community appears here in a new light; it goes far beyond a safeguarding of peace and liberty in his own community, and extends to communion with other communities, and with the regional and universal Church. The ecclesial ministry of leadership will also ensure that he does not become a cause of rupture rather than of support and unity.

Responsibility towards the Christian community is shown to be a responsibility to society in general. The leader of the Christian community will not, of course, act in a 'clerical' manner, by interfering in everything, even in matters in which he is wholly incompetent. He and his community will take part in the important questions of society: no particular party politics will prompt him here, but—*unambiguously*—the Christian message itself. This will occur less often than might be suspected by those whose partisan thought (whether of the left or the right) involves the Church in a struggle of opinions about political and social issues of the moment; those who make the Church a party, and want to put forward a specifically Christian 'solution' for each and every problem; but it occurs much more often than might be thought by those who would prefer to see the Church and its 'masters' confined to the sacristy, worship and private piety. Despite its intrinsic unity and inwardness, the Church is not a cultic association shuttered and withdrawn from the world. It is an open Church, aware of its commitment to the public, to other Christian Churches, but also to churchless Christians, the confession of the confessionless, of mankind as a whole. And the leader of the community bears the public responsibility for ensuring that the Church remains this communion in committed love —but here, and very particularly here, all bear the responsibility with him.

By his service of commitment in love, the leader leads the community: selflessly, and yet forcefully in his very commitment; reserved and yet decisive; both in public and in private constantly prompting and enlivening; but sometimes perhaps also holding back and moderating; never ceasing to refer to the gospel—that wholly unambiguous norm—for an ever-new future. For the leader of the community, this service of committed love must result from his service of word and sacrament. Only thus will he be able to escape the danger of being the only one who presides over worship in his community.

9. THE APOSTLE AS A MODEL FOR THE CHURCH LEADER

(*a*) By reason of the factors mentioned at the beginning, the image of the priest is in a full state of crisis, in the Catholic Church as elsewhere. Yet the ministry of leadership in the Church can exercise a certain attraction only if its image and the way it presents it are precisely defined, intact and convincing. All the evidence goes to show that the old sacralized image of the priest, inherited from the late Roman Empire, from Byzantium, from the Middle Ages and the post-Tridentine period, is no longer viable, either in theory or in practice. Today the younger a man is the more he tends to reject that kind of image. But it is all the more urgent, in a time that witnesses such an immense transformation of authority (not dissolution of authority), that in the Church too the 'new' image of the community leader, conceived on the basis of the New Testament and in terms of a new era, will be given a clear and precise outline; in this way it will gain in intensity and stability, so that a young man may once again identify with it (which is a matter of life and death for the Church).

The old image had a quite substantial content by reason of its relation to a specific social level: and one which appeared visibly, even in clothing and in the distinctive insignia proper to the rank in question. The new image has no such evocative power. It was very easy to draw a picture of a king; and a long time is needed before so clear and obvious an image will be available of the democratic leader. When it is a matter of forming and grasping something concretely, experience is as important as a theoretical analysis. An image has much more power and is much more forceful when it is lived than when it is merely drawn. History bears eloquent witness to this fact. Only the lived image can become a living and dynamic model.

But the church leader has available a lived original model with nothing sacred or authoritarian about it. This model has inspired countless people and has lost none of its illuminating strength for us today. On the contrary, compared with a traditional hierarch, it has a new luminance. What I have pointed out in regard to the essence of the service of the church leader is decisively important: it is a ministry dominated by the figure of the apostle Paul, himself moulded wholly by the person of Jesus Christ. Paul, by far the best-known figure of the primitive Church and the one who has exerted the greatest influence, understood more than all the others how to invite men to follow the faith and the creed of the apostles, their life and ministry. In particular he gave us from the start a clear idea of the man whose task it is to lead the Christian community. Of course Paul was more than a church leader: he was an apostle, one of the first witnesses to the living Christ, and he was aware of his apostolic mission and of its efficacy in the service of the gospel, which surpassed that of the other apostles. A reading of his epistles yields a dynamic model of the apostle intended precisely for a leader in the Church and the manner in which a leader must exercise authority. It is an image wholly on the lines of Jesus' own intention.

(*b*) This *dynamic apostolic model* of the church leader shows that Paul enjoyed enormous authority and acceptance within his churches, which depended on his human abilities but above all on the apostolic commission entrusted to him. He was never afraid to bring his authority into play. Yet it is characteristic of the Spirit of Christ that impelled Paul, that he did not exploit his mandatory power. He did not develop it so that it took the form of a relationship of sacral jurisdiction. Instead he always voluntarily restricted the exercise of his mandate in the conviction that the apostles were not lords and masters of the faith, but initiators of the joy of belief in all members of the community; that his churches belonged not to him but to the Lord; and that their members were free in the Spirit, called to be free and not slaves of men. Paul saw very clearly that his churches were lacking in maturity in many respects, and that they made mistakes. Yet his behaviour towards them was never that of a prudent teacher who has to educate his pupils before they can acquire liberty.

For Paul, liberty is the basic datum which he respects, and struggles for, so that his communities may follow him not out of constraint and force, but freely. Of course, where there was a risk of abandonment of Christ and his gospel in favour of another gospel, he had to use the threat of anathema and excommunication. But what he did in regard to an individual (temporary excommunication in the hope of an improvement) he never practised in respect of a community, even in cases of major deviations. Paul was always very careful to avoid using his mandatory power. Instead of issuing prohibitions, he appealed to individuals' judgment and responsibility. Instead of using constraint, he sought to convince. Instead of imposing himself, he exhorted. He said 'we . . .', not 'you . . .'; he did not issue sanctions but used forgiveness; and ultimately did not stifle but stimulated freedom.

Paul never abused his power in the sense of establishing a rule of man over man. On the contrary, in matters of ecclesial discipline he held back from decisions requiring the exercise of authority, even when it would have been quite justifiable. Similarly, when moral problems arose that did not pose a question concerning the Lord and his word, he left the communities their freedom rather than repress them. Even where the decision required seemed obvious, he avoided a unilateral move and brought in the community. Even though he was certainly authorized to intervene without appeal, he restrained himself and emphatically asked his communities not to force him to act. Even when he had a right, he preferred not to exercise it.

Essentially, then, Paul's relationship with his communities was neither that of a master nor that of a priest. Jesus is Lord and Master, and Jesus is the Lord who decides the norm for his Churches as for Paul. Even to treat his Christians as children is out of the question: they are his brothers, whom he serves in patience, courage and love. It is because he remains faithful to the service of the Lord —and not out of any human politeness or tact—that he is always ready to renounce the exercise of his mandatory power. He uses his mandate not to destroy but to instruct.

Paul did not pretend to be a superman. He was quite aware of his human limitations and did not claim infallibility. Peter, his closest counterpart in the New Testament, is always presented as the man who makes mistakes, is deficient, and goes back on his word. Each of the three classic texts that refer to the presence of Peter has some unusually violent contrast: the three solemn promises, for example, are countered by three grave inadequacies. All this should warn yet encourage the church leader today.

10. THE IMAGE OF THE CHURCH LEADER TODAY

It is an image essentially dependent on the dynamic apostolic model, which is oriented to Jesus. Nevertheless, in this time of change in authority and society, it has to be renewed. Everything positive that I have said up to now about the service of leadership in the Church, particularly in terms of essential functions—the service of the word, of the sacraments, and of the committed life—was directed to adapting this image concretely to our own times. The present one is no more than a general outline; for detailed, individual models we have to go to actual servants of the Church.

The outline gains in sharpness, intensity and life if we draw on the contemporary image of the democratic leader (John F. Kennedy, Martin Luther King, Dag Hammarskjöld—all three convinced Christians who are still living charismatic examples, precisely because they were assassinated while carrying out their service). How, on this basis, can we construct a model of the church leader in a democratic Church and society?

In view of certain trends in the social sciences and educational theory, which categorically reject (in a kind of opposition to authority) the authoritarian idea and the dynamic model, it will perhaps seem rather brash to try to make the image even more concrete. But I shall take the risk and hazard a few words, because (primarily) of all those throughout the Christian world who live such an image (in most cases effectively, even though they attract little attention and have all kinds of limitations); because, too, of all those (and they are not rare) who—with a little more confidence and commitment—could live up to such an image, or live up to it *better*. The following remarks will, I hope, reassure some and inspire others.

(*a*) A good church leader is also a man who proclaims the word in his community with authority. Of course he won't play God, and he will be aware of his human limitations, but he must know what is appropriate to his rôle. Many things that one might ascribe to a church leader are appropriate not in an exclusive but only in a positive sense. But they do concern him in a special way, inasmuch as he is the leader. If he does not do them, then often no one will, since no one feels impelled to. The leader becomes an authoritative (though not authoritarian) preacher not just because of the legitimacy he derives from his ordination, but by virtue of the inward authority he receives: in the proclamation of the word, the administration of the sacraments, and the committed service of love. He is a preacher not only in divine service (before God), but in human service (in relation to society). Something like an interpreter, simultaneously representing yet independent of the 'general will', he emphasizes the cause, the one needful thing, for which the community *is*, not only on behalf of this or that individual but *to* the (big or small) world, with energy, tenacity, intelligence, and imperturbability.

(*b*) A good church leader can *inspire*, *moderate* and *animate* his community. He will not imagine he is the Holy Spirit, but realize that his own flesh is weak and that he doesn't have to be a genius or an exemplary saint. The common cause will enable him to shine forth modestly and unpretentiously (modesty being interpreted now in a more comprehensive sense than the often romantic 'poverty'), despite all personal inadequacies. He will prompt and arouse. He will discover hidden talents and release new energies. By trusting others and enabling others to trust, he will be in a position to stimulate and fire them. A clear judgment and a readiness to take risks will help him to direct energies in the right direction and thus be an untiring *inspiration* to his community.

He must not confuse management and leadership, but cannot shun the work of organization. He will not just give orders but obtain his co-workers' approval for all major questions. He won't know the answer to everything himself, but will take trouble to search out the best, most detailed sources of information to help him tell adequate from inadequate solutions. And he won't want to do everything himself. Instead he will constantly make room for freedom, and see that other men's initiatives are encouraged. Very often he will just get things going, and co-ordinate forces. If possible he will intervene only in a subsidiary capacity: his care will be that things go well and that the human atmosphere of things is right; he will help to avoid tensions and resolve conflicts by fair means. In all this, he will be the prudent *moderator* of his community.

Since a moderator is the opposite of an agitator, he will be aware that neither bureaucratic routine nor fierce agitation is appropriate to the leader of the community. He must have a certain profundity to draw on if he is to be effective in a wide range of situations. He must know the traditions and values of the community if he is to face it with new tasks. In general, he must work to overcome individualistic interests, always keep reality and the community as a whole before his eyes, and try to achieve a multiform process of information and communication. In all this he will be something like the 'spirit' of the whole, and the *animator* of his community.

As inspirer, moderator and animator, in preaching the word and administering the sacraments, and in a committed service of love, he will keep the community together by constantly indicating its centre (without any bigotry or sentimental piety): by referring to Jesus as the Lord, and to the ultimate standard, the gospel; by working, too, on the basis of this centre and this norm, and trying in a critical spirit to establish relations between rival conceptions of the faith; by trying every way to peace and reconciliation, but also by pointing out, with imagination and common sense, means of common action within and without the community, so that it is kept together. In all this he will be the discreet and effective *spiritus rector* of his community.

(c) A good church leader can also become a *symbolic figure* for the community. Especially in large communities, men look for some personification of the ideas, values and aims of their group. The community leader is no messiah, and should not try to behave like one, even when he is successful. He must do his work without any false modesty, yet with a selfless realism and wholly unpretentious kind of rectitude. If a church leader is actually the inspirer, moderator and animator of his community, that is, the true *spiritus rector*; if, despite all his deficiencies in holiness, he is moved by the holy Spirit of Jesus Christ: then that which impels the community may take form in him, just as in a State the ideals of democracy may find an appropriate expression in the democratic leader. This does not mean that the church leader will be a kind of 'second Christ', and replace the first one. On the contrary, the marks I have described stress his connection with the one Christ and his message. The leader's lucidity will be apparent in his constant reference to Jesus Christ since his words, actions and way of life will make sure that the cause of Jesus Christ shines out. It is not his personal power of attraction that is decisive, whatever part it (necessarily) plays on this or that actual occasion. Instead his clear and unequivocal conviction, definite and unambiguous commitment, and greater openness and availability to the cause and to men make him a clear and shining light.

In this way, despite all his limitations, the church leader can become a symbolic figure for the community, who not only (like a specialist or expert) arouses men's understanding, observation, experience and reason, but by virtue of an authority emanating from his whole personality —both in his requirements and his assurances—appeals to their emotions, affectivity and passions—in short, to the whole man. For men need constantly to be stirred from comfort and slowness to change, and to be prompted to action and new commitment. But at the same time they need the consolation provided by someone who can assure them that they are on the right road, that they are able to take it, and can reach the goal. In this way the church leader will be the source not only of a salutary unease, but of help, energy and security, and thus inspire a greater readiness. He will not only provide a 'task' or 'instrumental' leadership, and—with his ideas and a certain degree of discipline—lead his community to a specific goal, but will supply 'social emotional' leadership in his concern for the cohesion of his community, by removing tensions, and by corroborating his community's high esteem for certain, definite ideals.

(d) The image of the church leader must be clear and appealing. But we must always remember that not every man will wholly satisfy this ideal since one will pay more attention to this basic function, and another will emphasize some other fundamental operation; one will bring out one basic trait, and another will stress some other characteristic; and so on. It is not essential that every church leader should be (to use Thomas Geiger's term) a 'thinker-for', 'arranger-for' and 'doer-for'—that is, a creative, organizational and technical wizard all at once. The church leader isn't everything at once; his vocation and his function *are only* one vocation and one function among many others of no lesser importance. All that I have said about the basic structure of the Church, which is charismatic, and in regard to the community of faith that unites free men and women as brothers and sisters with equal rights, is still true. I have had to concentrate on the function of the church leader, at the risk, perhaps, of giving it undue emphasis. As much could be said about the position and function of the teacher, theologian or prophet in the Church. The leader in the Church is not ultimately defined by his function and position in the Church, and certainly not by the power he might receive thereby, or any external prestige.

What is of decisive interest to the members of a (church or any other) group—the thing without which there can be no leadership, and whose absence produces an immediate credibility gap, is this: does the man at the top really believe what he says? Is he convinced that the way in which he preaches is the right way? Does he really think that the goal he puts before us is actually attainable? *Does he believe?* The question is posed even more radically for the leader of a *Christian community*. In this case, 'believing' means that he wholly trusts in and devotes himself to the Christian message, with all its theoretical and practical consequences—for him as well; that his whole existence is dedicated to Jesus and his cause. Only this personal *commitment in faith* (which need not be more closely elucidated here) can serve as the *basic principle* of the service of leadership in the Church.

This Christian commitment in faith can give the church leader the certitude and resolution that allow him to withstand anything: that special doubt that affects the thinker; the errors and failures that even the best will in the world cannot escape; the dangers and attacks that threaten a man in so exposed a position; all the (deserved or undeserved) blame that can so easily be put on him; and all the (deserved or undeserved) praise—which can be just as dangerous. This commitment in faith gives him the courage to suffer (which has always been part of the apostolic ministry and is far from unfruitful for the Christian) and—and this is said without any false sentiment—the courage to bear the Cross. More than for many others, his way in the service of the gospel and of mankind is a way of the Cross: which for every Christian is a sign that he has been chosen as a follower of Christ.

What matters for the leader of a Church (whether small and insignificant or great and important) is not, ultimately, the position or prestige accorded him, but whether and to what extent he simply and honestly *believes*: whether, that is, together with all others in this community of free men and women and equally entitled brothers and sisters, he *believes*, *loves* and *hopes*.

And so we are back at our starting point. But only practice will show whether what seems to be valid in theory is really effective. The crisis of the Church and its service of leadership today will be overcome by those who, at this decisive moment in the Church's history, *despite everything* perform their service in the strength of faith.

Also available in
the Fontana Library of Theology and Philosophy

Evil and the God of Love
JOHN HICK
'The tone of the book is magnificent. It is the most exciting work of its kind that I have read for several years.' *John Raymond, Sunday Times*

Evolution: The Theory of Teilhard de Chardin
BERNARD DELFGAAUW
Written in clear and simple language, this book gives a new insight into Teilhard's thinking on this ever topical subject. It has already gone into 12 editions in Holland.

The Death of Christ
JOHN KNOX
'His preaching of the Cross has a power denied to the Nicene Creed and to the best of the commentaries on it.' *Times Literary Supplement*

Love Almighty and Ills Unlimited
AUSTIN FARRER
'One of the most acute theological minds of the day, master of a scintillating style. The book is intellectually brilliant. The verbal and mental fireworks explode and glitter on page after page.' *Church Times*

Also available in
the Fontana Library of Theology and Philosophy

No Rusty Swords
DIETRICH BONHOEFFER
'Anyone who would really know the man who wrote the *Letters and Papers from Prison* must first follow the struggles and development of the young Bonhoeffer outlined in this book.' *Times Educational Supplement*

Love and Marriage
EMIL BRUNNER
'A solid, coherent treatment. Mr Sproxton supplies an interesting introduction to Brunner's thought and chooses the chapters from the original work (*The Divine Imperative*) wisely.' *Tablet*

Language, Logic and God
FREDERICK FERRÉ
'Deals with genuine issues of our time. The book is very good value, especially for students.' *Church of England Newspaper*

Our Experience of God
H. D. LEWIS
'We can do no more than call attention to the inestimable service he has rendered by the scholarly and liberal spirit in which he has treated some of the leading problems in the philosophy of religion.' *Times Literary Supplement*